KEEPING YOUR TEEN IN TOUCH WITH GOD

*Why teens turn away
from the church
and how you can prevent it*

Dr. Robert Laurent

D0815943

David C. Cook Publishing Co.
Elgin, Illinois•Weston, Ontario
Nova Distribution Ltd. Torquay, England

LifeJourney Books is an imprint of David C. Cook
Publishing Co.
David C. Cook Publishing Co., Elgin, Illinois 60120
David C. Cook Publishing Co., Weston, Ontario
Nova Distribution Ltd., Torquay, England

KEEPING YOUR TEEN IN TOUCH WITH GOD
©1988 by Robert Laurent

Edited by LoraBeth Norton
Book design by Dawn Lauck
Cover design by Stephen D. Smith
Cover illustration by Anita Nelson

First paperback printing, 1991
Printed in the United States of America
95 94 93 92   5 4 3 2
Laurent, Robert
        Keeping Your Teen in Touch with God
        Bibliography: p. 155
        Includes Index
        1. Youth—Religious Life. I. Title
        ISBN 1-55513-558-7

CONTENTS

DEDICATED TO

my wife and best friend, Joyce

my four favorite teens and pre-teens,
Christopher, Holly, Laura, and Joy

my "boss" and the finest academic dean in the country,
Harold Harper

my neighbor, colleague, and friend, Richard Besancon,
whose heart for students and the Lordship of Jesus Christ
has been a constant inspiration to me.

FOREWORD

By Jay Kesler
President of Taylor University

I HAVE BEEN OF THE OPINION FOR some time that the role of the youth worker is to be an interpreter. He or she must interpret youth to adults and adults to youth. In order to do this, one has to have had some experience at being both. Many very young youth workers are able to help young people because they can identify with the struggles the teens are having with their parents. Many, however, have not worked through their own relationships well enough to fairly portray the complexities of the parent-teen relationship.

Unfortunately, many youth workers leave youth work before these issues are resolved and, though they have provided a form of empathetic commiseration, their ministry has little in it that would not have been provided by a thoughtful peer. This is not all bad, of course, and indeed much good comes of these ministries.

Bob Laurent has stayed with youth work over the long haul. He started preaching very early and grew as his experience broadened. He also worked hard to add to his formal education. These facts, combined with a loyalty to the home and church, have made his ministry a lasting one. Now, in this book, he passes on to parents, youth workers, and young people the combined insights of his considerable experience. Few have given more diligence to the task, and it shows.

The issues discussed in these pages are real and important. They are the concerns of young people and parents and, therefore, are intensely practical. I doubt if we can ever have too many thoughtful, practical, readable books on this topic. I hope that those who read this book pass it on, with their endorsement, to others who will be helped. So very many of the heartaches in the parent-teen relationship are avoidable if only parents can apply humility, patience, understanding, prayer, and consistency to the task.

This book makes practical suggestions that all can apply with confidence. Bob Laurent is poised and experienced for the task of interpreter, and his message is clearly communicated.

PREFACE

SHUFFLING ALONG THE SMORGASBORD line as guest speaker at a men's service club luncheon, I silently prayed that God would direct my thoughts as I prepared to address these upwardly-mobile, worldly-wise businessmen. The random noises around the salad bar did little to inspire me.

"Hey, Tom! Those Cardinals beat your Cubbies again last night! Why don't you root for a real major league team?"

"I heard gas prices will skyrocket this weekend. Oil's up ten dollars a barrel."

"Did you guys see the new waitress? On a scale of one to ten, that woman's got to be an eleven!"

As the cacophony of meaningless talk drifted to the crowded tables, one beleaguered voice caught my attention: "I don't know what more I can do for her! I've given her everything! She's not the only dumb kid who ever got pregnant—but she's mine!"

Embarrassed by his outburst, or perhaps vexed by the unresponsive friend on his left, the man grew quiet, absently using a fork to rearrange the food on his plate. He balanced his black-framed glasses on the end of his nose and murmured," I just don't understand her. We even tried religion, and that didn't help!"

I knew then what I had to speak about. It has always puzzled me that many men exhibit visible shame after failing at business, but maintain almost a cavalier attitude about failing at home. In a way, the troubled man just a few seats away was a refreshing change. I felt a Christ-centered compassion for him and the rest of those in attendance who obviously understand how to make a living, but—like so many of us parents of teenagers—had something more to learn about how to live.

I told them of a God who loved them and who was willing to forgive both them and their children; a Father-God whose highest hope was to bring harmony to their families through faith in His Son, Jesus Christ. Purposely misquoting Mark 8:36 (and trusting the Author would understand), I spoke on this topic: "What Does it Profit a Businessman to Gain the Whole World and Lose His Own Family?"

None of us needs to feel alone or helpless when our teenagers seem to turn against us. The truth is that even very religions parents often raise rebellious children. It is not unusual for children to reject the faith and values of their parents when they reach adolescence.

It is a fact that over fifty percent of Christian teenagers will sit in church next Sunday morning. Within two years, seventy percent of them will have left the church, never to return. What are the reasons behind this mass exodus?

Gallup polls report that forty percent of all teenagers believe in astrology, thirty percent read astrology columns daily, and ninety-three percent know their astrological sign. Gallup further reveals that sixty-five percent of evangelical teens never read their Bibles and thirty-three percent feel that religion is out-of-date and out-of-touch.[1]

A survey conducted by Wheaton College in conjunction with Campus Crusade for Christ disclosed that there is less than a ten percent difference in moral beliefs between churched and non-churched students.[2] It seems obvious that the Gospel of Jesus Christ is making little difference in the lives of many teenagers.

Catholic University in Washington, D.C. directed a study among Christian teens and found that thirty-two percent of Catholic youth, thirty-four percent of Baptist, and twenty-five percent of Methodist teenagers admit to the need for religion but "cannot relate to the present church."[3]

There is one phenomenon I have never quite been able to get over: those promising teens who "try religion" for a while and then turn their backs on their parents and on the church. Few things cause me more grief than to see an adolescent whom I have come to love reject the Christian values which mean so much to me.

I determined to target these teens for research and ministry. In doing so, I have learned some crucial principles regarding adolescent alienation from religion. There are reasons that many teenagers in the church reject Christianity— reasons which need to be examined, discussed, and acted upon. But there is very little Christian literature available that is based on solid, empirical research dealing with this important topic. Where do parents go for help?

This book is, in part, an answer to that need.

CHAPTER

1

Insanity Is Contagious

You Can Get It from Your Teenager

I KNOW A FAMILY WITH FIVE teenagers! Can you imagine? Five astonishing appetites to reduce Mom from a planner of nutritious meals to a short order cook and leave Dad staring into a basket emptied of blueberry muffins by the time it gets around to him!

With five teens, would there ever be any milk left in the refrigerator? Would there ever be an open phone line, a hairbrush in the bathroom, or a chance to wear your own clothes? Would the car insurance bill ever be under $800? With five teens, would there ever be a time when you felt comfortable letting your neighbors see the inside of your house?

And while we're on the subject of houses, whoever builds them doesn't have most teens in mind. A family with teenagers needs a bigger garage for the driver's training years, bigger bathrooms for all those cosmetic experiments, and bigger bedrooms so the walls can accommodate an even one hundred posters.

I have another great idea for the bedrooms as well. You know how some fireplaces have trapdoors for getting rid of the ashes? Every teenager's bedroom should be equipped with two such doors, one on each side of the room. One would be designated for clothing and open directly over the washing machine in the basement. The second would be for fungi-bearing piles of food wrappers, Popsicle sticks, banana peels, apple cores, and other biodegradable items and could open over a well-contained incinerator. There is a possible drawback to the scheme: while stumbling about in a semi-waking stupor some morning, your confused teen might wind up incinerating his clothing and laundering his Twinkies wrappers.

Be encouraged. Most of you will never have to raise five teenagers at the same time. Still, there is no doubt that parenting even one teenager is a special challenge and, many experts would have us believe, a war of attrition that cannot be won. Almost every textbook I've read on adolescent psychology labels the teenage period as one of "storm and stress."

Mark Twain's quip, "When a boy reaches thirteen, put him in a barrel and feed him through the knothole—and when he gets to sixteen, plug up the knothole!" has been taken to heart by many Americans. When my own family was younger, I was warned by many good-intentioned friends, "Enjoy your children while they're young. When they get older, they'll break your heart."

And I agree that as your family grows, so does the risk of being hurt by your children. The chances for painful conflict seem to multiply in direct proportion to your son's fixation with cars and your daughter's contribution to the phone bill. I have often wondered why, in God's economy, teenagers start getting pimples just about the same time that Dad begins to grow up through his hair and Mom watches her figure add new dimensions to her life. I mean, how much stress can a family take?

Yes, there is a good chance that your teenager might hurt

you (or perhaps already has). You would not be the first Christian parent whose adolescent daughter became pregnant, or whose son was arrested for drinking or possession of drugs. Your first reaction might have been to worry about your own reputation in the church or community. You might even have been tempted to let roots of bitterness and anger grow up within you, putting a great strain on your relationship with your teen. But by now, perhaps, you have learned that taking your own "pain pulse" is self-defeating. Maybe the question shouldn't be, "How much has my teen hurt me?" but "How much do I hurt for my teen?"

Hope for the Family

While it is true that God loves us and often gives us a second chance with our children, He also expects us to be prepared the best we can to help our teens do more than merely survive their adolescence. I know that you love your teenager, and that is one reason that there is great hope for your family.

Christian parents can have a powerful impact on their teens via a twofold influence:

a) a preventative influence, in which the parents learn to equip their teens to face the special challenges and pressures that will confront them during these critical years, and

b) a redemptive influence, in which the parents can learn to demonstrate the reconciling love of God by helping to restore their teens both to Christian standards and back into the family unit.

I have never gotten over the exciting truth of II Corinthians 5:15: "And He died for all, that those who live should no longer live for themselves but for Him who died for them and was raised again."

The phrase "should no longer live for themselves" was

11

written to teenagers as well as to self-actualized adults. The good news is that at that developmental stage when teens are struggling through the most self-centered time of their lives, they are also wonderfully open to a life-changing experience with Jesus Christ. Teenagers make great Christians. Their faith is spontaneous and contagious. Their passion for Christ revives us; their fresh testimony takes us back to our spiritual roots; their honesty forces us to look at our own motives for being Christians.

I have said for years that one crucial sign of a healthy church is a youth program with life and commitment. I have come to believe that the same is true of the Christian family. A dedicated Christian teenager can have a remarkable effect on the harmony of the home.

I hope that this book will fulfill the following objectives:

1) help parents to understand the unique emotional and spiritual needs of their teens.

2) assist parents in opening up lines of communication with their teenagers.

3) offer specific answers to everyday teen/parent problems.

4) give fresh, Biblical insights for leading teens into an active involvement with Christianity.

5) discuss the reasons that teens, even good "church kids," reject their religion and choose destructive alternatives.

6) provide creative ways for parents to promote the acceptance of Christian values by their teens.

7) point the way to stronger love relationships between parents and their teenagers.

A Christian family led by parents who are open to learning how to understand and help their teens can handle anything. The fact that you've picked up this book indicates that kind of openness on your part.

CHAPTER
2

The Reasons Teens Reject Religion

RICHARD WAS A THICK-SET BOY with broad shoulders and a shock of blond hair which he kept brushing out of his eyes. Sitting near the back of the room, alternately staring at the floor or whispering to the girl next to him, he made it clear that he was not at the youth retreat to listen to me speak. He had heckled me during an earlier session, and when I tried to talk with him about his belligerent attitude, he scowled and walked away.

I finished my message, passed out paper and pencils, and asked the teens to help me get a sense for where they were by describing how they felt about their religion. I encouraged them to take their time and think about their answers before they wrote. Richard grabbed a pencil and quickly scrawled out his response. It was not difficult later for me to figure out who had written in bold, capital letters: "I HATE IT!"

Richard is not alone among churched teens in his anger toward all that "religion" has come to represent. I remember another tense scene that occurred when I was speaking in southern California. Standing by a tree outside the church just before the evening service, I noticed a teenaged boy and his mother walking toward me. When she stopped at the door to the sanctuary and waited for her son to open it for her, he began to shout.

"Mom, this isn't fair! You tricked me! You said you were taking me to a concert!"

She looked around, embarrassed, and replied, "That's what it is. There's a music group inside." (She didn't mention that I would be preaching after the music.)

Incensed by her reply, the boy yelled even louder:

"This is not a concert! This is a church, and I told you I would never go back to church!"

These two examples may be somewhat extreme, but the negative attitudes about the church typify some youth of every denomination. For several years I have been asking teens in churches across the country to finish the sentence, "My feelings when I think of my religion are. . . ." Too many of the responses reveal that some teenagers are choosing against their religion:

> . . . *hate and sadness. The door that Jesus was beating on I now keep locked.*
>
> *I don't follow it!*
>
> *It can drag you down.*
>
> *Talk to me about the real world—not Christianity!*
>
> *I don't think that I can handle Christianity at this point in my life.*
>
> *I'm not interested in the church much at all. My parents are, but I'd rather be me.*
>
> *I think it's all screwed up!*
>
> *My Christian life is the pits! I go to church and everything, but I don't ever get anything out of it.*

BREAKING AWAY

In a 1980 study of people who have left the church, David Roozen estimated that forty-six percent of Americans withdraw from active religious participation at some point in their lives. He found that this rate was greatest among adolescents.[1]

In the early and middle teenage years, there are many symptoms of alienation from religion. Your teens might begin to complain about having to go to church so often.

Nobody goes as much as we do. We live at the church!

They may question the most basic traditions of your religious family life-style.

Please don't ask me to pray when my friends eat with us. It's embarrassing.

You can expect them to grumble about your standards regarding music, television, and movies.

You had your music when you were our age. Why can't we listen to our rock music? (You will be tempted to reply, "Because Frankie Avalon didn't bite a live bat's head off during his performance.")

Or have you heard this one?

Why can't I go to that movie? The PG-13 rating means that anybody thirteen years old is supposed to see it!

There are many comments which might indicate your teen's disenchantment with religion, but the one you can almost count on hearing will be: Do we have to go to church? It's so boring!

Older teens who are breaking away from parental restraint or young adults who get out on their own may throw off all pretense of being religious. A friend of mine, now in his mid-thirties, told me of a major encounter with his father that he had during his high school days. In the fever of battle, his dad issued an emotional ultimatum that has been sounded in many Christian homes: "As long as you live under this roof, you will never drink, and you will always go to church!" It's easy to predict the first two areas in which he, upon graduation from high school, defied his father.

It is true that some youth who leave the church may find their way back to a personal faith in Jesus Christ. But for too many, the rejection will be permanent.

FOUR TYPES OF TEENS

Many years ago I stayed in the home of a Christian family with three teenagers. Two of them seemed to have stepped out of a *Moody Monthly* advertisement for choir robes. They were bright and friendly, attending all of the special meetings that week at their church. But the third, a sixteen-year-old daughter, was determined to break the world record for rebellious acts during a revival. As I listened to her scream at her parents, cursing them with words I hadn't heard since the church league basketball tournament, I wondered how the same family could produce such diverse children.

The truth is that each of our teens is unique; understanding that may be our first step in helping them. Proverbs 22:6 counsels us to "train up a child in the way he should go," indicating that each child has been created with a distinct personality and temperament, and you may have to vary your methods of leading them into the Christian faith.

There are at least four types of church-related teenagers. The first, like the young lady with the sailor's vocabulary, are verbally and visibly alienated from religion. Perhaps they once embraced the church, but for some reason their experience with religion has been so negative that they have completely withdrawn from it.

They seem to enjoy being critical of anything or anyone religious. They may even try to live in open rebellion against their parents. The trappings of religion seem to take the joy out of the present. Like hand-me-down clothing, the religion of their parents just doesn't seem to fit anymore.

At age seventeen, I was the second type of teen. Never

openly hostile, I was alienated from and inwardly critical of religion, but wouldn't dare express it for fear of the consequences. I was expected to be at church and, under the watchful eyes of my parents, I did my duty. I was expected to get good grades and never to smoke, drink, or "party." I was expected to sing solos during worship service and be an active participant in all church functions, and I met those expectations.

In retrospect, I see that I had never experienced a constitutional change, had never allowed Jesus Christ to make me into a new creation. I was not an inner-directed person, controlled by the Holy Spirit. Rather, my behavior was dictated by the expectations of others, making me one of those miserable unfortunates who have enough religion to bother them but never to bless them.

I learned early what it took to gain the praise and approval of my parents and other authority figures, and my performance was flawless. Knowing that I was false eventually led me to despise not only myself, but also those who I felt were compelling me to perform.

Although I had my share of perfect attendance pins throughout high school, I think I knew then that once I graduated, I would no longer go to church. Most of my friends at the university were not Christians, and there was no way I was going to live by Christian standards among a non-Christian peer group.

The third type is perhaps the most common religious teenager. These are the adolescents who often produce the most anxiety and discouragement in youth pastors and reduce their ministry to glorified baby-sitting. They are fairly regular in attendance, but don't really care about the church. Their faith is marked by apathy and disinterest in the church's real mission. This teen is content, for the time being, to sing "Just As I Am" while he remains just as he is.

I have met the fourth type of religious teenager in high

schools and churches nationwide. While not as common as the religiously apathetic teens, the vibrancy of their faith makes them very visible. They sit in the front row at the youth meeting with open Bibles and looks of expectancy on their faces. They ask me to pray with them for a non-Christian friend. I agree and listen reverently as they pour out their hearts to a God who is obviously a close, personal friend.

They are deeply concerned about personal holiness and seek to make Jesus Christ as much a part of their dating life as their church life. They may not understand or accept everything that the church teaches, but they internalize what they do understand and are caught up in the life and mission of the church.

These teenagers are not typical, but they are becoming less rare as a grass-roots spiritual renewal continues to spread among American youth. In a recent summer over 10,000 teens showed up at the Youth Congress on Evangelism in Washington, D.C. to receive intensive training for sharing their faith with others. During Christmas vacation of that same year, the Wesleyans hosted a four-day conference, inviting only teens who were serious about becoming active disciples of the Lord Jesus Christ. Over 6,000 young people packed into the University of Illinois Assembly Hall to receive instruction in discipleship.

Discussing a survey conducted by *Teen* magazine, Judith Marks stated,

> *"Whether they're discovering their own spirituality for the first time or simply redefining it, young people appear to be returning to organized religion in ever-increasing numbers. A recent survey of our readership confirms this trend. Ninety-six percent of the teens polled believe in God, and 80.8 percent rate religion as an important or extremely important part of their lives."*[2]

In my own survey I received many positive responses to the statement, "My feelings when I think of my religion are. . . ."

God is very special to me. He is my life.

My feelings are great because God is first in my life, and I couldn't live without Him. I owe Him everything for making me the way I am today.

God is a real and personal friend in my life. He cares for me and hears me when I speak to Him.

I feel excited because I know the love of Christ. I am happy and warm inside because I love God and I love my religion.

DYING FOR A REASON TO LIVE

Every teenager should have the chance to make these kinds of statements, to have an intimate, life-giving friendship with Jesus Christ. But most teens no longer automatically accept the religion of their families. The uniformity that once almost guaranteed that a teenager's religious values and choices of friends would be extensions of family values has largely eroded.

Some youth, in turning away from the purpose that Christianity could give them, face the ultimate in despair. Over 5,000 teens kill themselves every year. According to Charlotte Ross, director of the Youth Suicide National Center in Washington, D.C., over half a million others try but fail. Suicide is now the second major cause of death among adolescents.[3]

Only now can Elaine Hoff, of the Illinois Attorney General's Office, talk publicly about her son, Scott, a gifted student who was elected vice-president of his seventh grade class. On October 15, 1985, Scott hanged himself. He was thirteen.

"We still do not know why our son chose to die by

suicide," Hoff says. "What happened will never be okay. Our life is changed forever. . . . So I guess you always repeat that question—Why? Why?—because it shouldn't be."[4]

Mrs. Hoff is right. It shouldn't be.

REMOVING THE BARRIERS

In their book, *Reaching Youth Today,* Hargrove and Jones are exactly right when they say that faith in Jesus Christ can equip a teen with "a sense of purpose which appeals to the idealistic, providing a strong sense of identity and self-worth."[5] Helping parents to remove the barriers which keep their teens from a vibrant Christian faith is the major purpose of this book.

But before a difficult problem can be solved, it must be understood. Therefore, I set out to identify and isolate specific reasons that cause teens to reject religion. From years of experience in counseling teenagers and their parents, I recognized the same factors surfacing again and again.

Based on Roger Dudley's "Youth Perceptual Inventory,"[6] I devised a 167-item questionnaire in which I included those ten recurring themes and asked teens from all over the country to choose those factors which caused them to reject religion. The results of the questionnaire are revealed in this book, with the ten major causes for teenage rejection of religion dealt with in the order that the teens themselves ranked them.

Before you read further, it might be interesting for you to rank the ten causes yourself. Also, score them the way you think the teens in the survey did, giving a 1 to the cause that you believe would most cause a teenager to reject his religion, a 2 to the second highest cause, and so on.

CAUSES OF TEENAGE REJECTION OF RELIGION

MY GUESS	TEENS' RANKING	
_____	_____	Lack of opportunity for church involvement
_____	_____	Negative media influence (TV, rock music, movies)
_____	_____	Poor relationship with parents
_____	_____	Low self-esteem
_____	_____	Poor relationship with youth pastor
_____	_____	Negative peer influence
_____	_____	Authoritarianism in parents
_____	_____	The struggle for emancipation from parents
_____	_____	Negative concept of religion
_____	_____	Lack of family harmony

(Actually, the ten causes are listed here in order of the teens' ranking. How did you do?)

I interviewed over 400 randomly selected high school students. From the beginning, I intended for this study to meet the requirements of the scientific method. Whereas much of the literature regarding teens and religion is characterized by conjecture and personal opinion, this study offers empirical evidence on a subject about which there has been little scientific research.

This study goes beyond external observation to probe the attitudes and innermost feelings of the teens who were surveyed. For example, although withdrawal from the church may indicate alienation, it could be very misleading to assume the opposite. Just because your teen is keeping up his attendance and showing all the external signs of being a "good church kid" doesn't mean that serious alienation is not present.

Finally, this study is needed because it really listens to the teens. Many youth are so accustomed to one-way communications from adults that any opportunity they have to express their feelings takes on real significance. As you will see, the teenagers interviewed expressed their feelings. Their answers were direct, often emotionally charged, and very revealing. They had some important things to say to us about what causes them to reject Christianity and what we can do to help them grow in their faith.

CHAPTER

3

Let My Young People Go

Reason #1: Lack of opportunity for church involvement

MANY TEENAGERS BELIEVE that there is no place for them in the church. In my study, the lack of opportunity for church involvement proved to be the number one reason teens eventually reject religion. Over seventy-five percent of the youth who demonstrated a general, across-the-board alienation from religion indicated that the church's failure to take them seriously and include them in significant roles is the major cause of their estrangement.

There are many reasons that our teens are leaving the church, and we parents cannot afford to be reductionists by focusing on just a few of them. Still, if there was only one barrier that I could remove, it would be the lack of opportunity for church involvement. Teens who are not actively involved in a church role that they perceive as important care very little for religion. Simply stated, if they are not a part of it, they will probably depart from it. Teens need to be needed.

If they don't feel valuable, they won't stop, look, or listen for long. They will either leave the church or simply put in their time there, waiting for the chance to be with a peer group, whatever its standards, where they will be made to feel important.

I asked the teens in the survey to respond to several items which would reveal what they thought their present role in the church was. For each item they could mark "strongly agree," "agree somewhat," "undecided," "disagree somewhat," or "strongly disagree." Again and again, the teens registered their discouragement and belief that the church's need for them was simply nonexistent.

"I feel I'm an important part of the ministry of our church." (strongly disagree)

"I'm not good enough for God to use me." (agree)

"I'd be shocked if someone asked me to do something important at my church." (strongly agree)

"I'm seriously considering going into full-time Christian service." (strongly disagree)

"I have a lot of opportunities for service in my church." (strongly disagree)

THERE'S STILL A COST

I began my Christian life in 1967 at age twenty. The late 60s-early 70s was a fertile period for lofty goals and rampant idealism. Everyone had a cause to fight for in those days. Teenagers proudly brandished their new identity: the "tell-it-like-it-is" generation. They burned their draft cards while fighting pollution, racism, the war in Vietnam, and the tottering establishment.

It is no wonder that the generation which sought truth in a world that produced Watergate and demanded absolutes in a society morally enervated by situation ethics would find

Jesus Christ. The penniless revolutionary from Nazareth, the King of the Universe impaled on a cross out of love for a world gone mad, found a ready following among teenagers disillusioned with antiseptic religion and impersonal authority figures.

When Hollywood spawned occult movies like Rosemary's Baby and The Exorcist, aroused cadres of Christian teens from the "Jesus people" of California to the sanctified street gangs of New York City enlisted to do battle against Satan himself.

But where the adolescents of the 60s battled for a cause, today's teens are battling for a job. There was a time when teens eschewed materialism and marched against injustice and compromise. The modern teen seems to have made peace with the establishment and joined the gold rush to financial prosperity.

When Jim Elliot, Nate Saint and three other courageous missionaries surrendered their lives to the Auca spears in 1956, thousands of teens and young adults surrendered their lives to the mission field. Today, we think it remarkable if a teenager surrenders a few dollars of his paycheck to the offering plate.

I heard a Christian teen describing to her girlfriend the beautiful new wardrobe she had just purchased for the coming school year. Her friend was obviously impressed, but complained that she could never afford such extravagance. The girl with the new clothes replied, "Sure you can. Just use my shopping philosophy: 'Mastercharge it and pray for the Rapture!'"

Jesus Christ still faces teenagers with an unequivocal challenge to join the company of the fully committed. He does not offer a religion of accommodation and expediency. His voice is a clarion call, and we parents dare not dilute His mandate:

"If any [teen] would come after me, let him deny

himself, and take up his cross daily, and follow me" (Luke 9:23).

"Any [teen] who does not give up everything he has cannot be my disciple" (Luke 14:33).

"Whatever [teen] loses his life for my sake will find it" (Matthew 10:39).

Could it be that in our efforts to make sure that our children have it better than we did, we have unwittingly stripped them of the only thing that can keep their faith strong in the first place: an uncompromising commitment to the Lordship of Jesus Christ that fuels itself via active participation in the ministry of the church?

Offering them a religion that merely entertains and cajoles them might ensure their attendance for awhile, but it does not prepare them for the pressing demands of the real world. Pampering our teens with a steady diet of amusement parks and trips to the beach might add a few numbers to the youth group, but it does not equip them to help others or themselves, and inexorably leads to their rejection of religion. The data from this study and experience itself support this thesis.

In the spiritual sense, then, it may be the wise parents who want their children to have it tougher than they had it. I've recently been reading Donald Sloat's book, *The Dangers of Growing Up in a Christian Home*. In the chapter, "God Has No Grandchildren," he says,

> *Each of us is different and has to come to grips with his own faith and make it real through personal experience. We as parents need to realize this point and allow our children to have experiences from which they can learn, not overly sheltering them. This is probably one of the hardest things for us to do because we love our children and do not want to see them experience pain or failure.*[1]

By baptizing our teens in things, we have helped them to develop "marshmallow" philosophies of life. Not needing to make hard choices, they are conditioned to postpone difficult decisions and repress glimpses of their own character flaws. In our efforts to give them pleasure, we have rendered them useless for dealing with pain.

The irony is that most teens who have been doted on have had little opportunity to develop their wills and often become easy targets for drugs and other seducers. Our upward mobility and pursuit of that illusive American dream seems to have worn thin on both generations, and left all of us wondering how so much wealth could cause so much emptiness.

WHEN FAITH COMES HOME

If I needed convincing that teenagers need opportunities to be used by God for their faith to become real to them, it came last year. I had been concerned about my twelve-year-old Holly's lack of enthusiasm for church and was praying regularly for God to energize her faith.

One day she arrived home from school with an ugly scratch across her face. I admit that I am an overly protective father and will never be accused of being too gentle with anyone who harms one of my children. My natural instincts were engaged.

"What happened, Holly? Who hurt you?!"

"Oh, it's okay, Dad," she replied. "It was just dumb Brian."

"Who is dumb Brian?" I queried. "Where does he live?"

"He's just a nerd, Dad. You know—a geek. He didn't mean to hurt me. He just stretched to yawn or something, and he's such a klutz that he scratched my face."

I was scheduled to speak in Holly's class in two days. Several of the students' fathers had already been invited to talk to the class about their jobs; Thursday was the "preacher-dad's" turn. I determined to look up "dumb Brian."

As I spoke from behind the teacher's desk, I wondered if Holly would give me any indication of where Brian was seated. God couldn't have been very pleased with me that day. Even as I told the students how much He loved them, my eyes were tracking up and down the rows, trying to figure out which of those boys hurt my little girl.

Back home that afternoon, I watched Holly get off the bus. She ran up the driveway, waving an envelope. I asked what her friends thought of my talk but, as if she didn't even hear me, she pushed the envelope into my hand.

"Dad, Brian told me to give this to you."

I opened the note and read,

Dear Mr. Laurent,

Please pray for me, sir. My parents are getting a divorce. And I'm thinking about suicide. Thank you very much.

Brian Daniels—age 12

Many people believe that most teenagers threaten suicide but never act on it. I've learned otherwise—the hard way. Feeling guilty, I stared at his letter for a difficult moment. I hadn't been praying for that boy. In fact, I had gone to his class more to prey on him than pray for him.

Needing help, I instinctively turned to Holly. I handed her the suicide note and watched her eyes widen as she read. My daughter knew that Brian was dead serious and blurted out, "Dad, he's going to kill himself! What are we going to do? We'd better pray for him!"

God was answering my prayer for Holly's faith to come alive. We went to her bedroom and knelt together by her bed. Before this, I had always initiated any of our prayer times together. Now she was in control, with the incisiveness that desperation brings to prayer.

"God, don't let Brian do it," she pleaded, her tears punctuating each sentence. "Show him how much You love him. Please, Lord, give him a reason to live. And if You want to," she added, "use me to help."

We stood up and embraced. It was a special moment. I knew that something extraordinary was going to happen at her school.

When she arrived at the door of her classroom the next morning, she was greeted by several of the bigger boys in class.

"Hey, Holly. Guess what we're doing today? You're gonna love it," they announced. Thinking it would impress her, they boasted, "We're gonna beat up dumb Brian. What a nerd! He's got it coming!"

What they were not aware of was that God had changed Holly's heart regarding Brian. Her defiance was prompt.

"You guys better not touch him. If you do, I'll go to the principal!"

"C'mon, Holly," they challenged. "You hate him as much as we do. You wouldn't dare tell on us!"

"Oh, yeah?" she countered. "Just watch me!"

Later at recess, Holly invited Brian to play tag with her and another girl. She said that his face positively lighted up.

"Who, me?" he asked. "You bet!"

Things were going great until Brian tripped over a snow drift and collided with Abby, the biggest girl in the sixth grade, and one of Holly's best friends. Abby towered over him and screamed for everyone to hear, "Watch where you're going, jerk!"

As Brian lay there, spread-eagled in the snow, looking up at his furious adversary, Holly had no trouble reading his thoughts: "You're absolutely right. That's my name: jerk, nerd, geek, idiot. And I'm going to kill myself."

Fighting for a cause can galvanize any teenager to noble actions. Not thinking about the consequences, and prompted by God's Spirit, Holly jumped between the two of them.

"He didn't mean to do it, Abby. It was an accident."

Abby rounded on her, demanding, "What's your problem, Holly? Do you like him or something?"

I have often wondered what my response would have been at that moment. Knowing my cowardly nature and maladjusted urge to please everyone during my school years, I probably would have replied, "Aw, leave him alone, Abby. He's just a geek anyway. He's not worth wasting your time on."

But because it was so unexpected, Holly's answer became the talk of her classroom that day.

"Yeah," she challenged. "He's my friend."

That response was significant for two reasons. First of all, Brian heard it. Someone valued him. He was on the road to emotional healing. Secondly, Holly heard herself say it, and with that conscious decision to controvert the spirit of the world, obey God, and show Brian the love of Jesus Christ, her own faith took on a depth that simply had not been there before.

The next day, she and I had the privilege of sharing the plan of salvation with Brian over a cheeseburger. He is now a member of God's "forever family."

But just as important, Holly will never be the same again. She knows that God did something important through her that day, and the experience has given an intentionality to her faith. She got a taste for the excitement and danger of living on the mission level, and like most teens who experience this phenomenon, she is not really happy or satisfied unless God is using her.

READY FOR HIGH PLACES

You will not have to drag to church the teen who is excited about being needed by God. You will not have to coax or trick him into going to the church's youth functions. On the contrary, you'll be tempted to leave your car keys on top of his Bible.

Christian teens sense that they should be doing something for God. If we give them no opportunity to get involved, there is a good chance we will lose them. A recent Gallup survey on religion in America reported that most Americans believe the country is facing a "moral crisis of the first dimension, that society is failing to meet the spiritual needs of youth, and that young people want somehow, in some way, to serve."[2]

In Psalm 18, God gives parents a clue about His plans for our teens, as well as for us: "It is God who arms me with strength and makes my way perfect. He makes my feet like the feet of a mountain goat. He enables me to stand on high places. He trains my hands for battle" (vv. 32-34a).

Teenagers love to do battle. Along with a keen eye for hypocrisy, they seem to have a built-in capacity for high adventure. I co-led a tour of sixty teens and adults to Israel several years ago. We made the mistake of traveling northward from Jerusalem to Samaria on June 6, the anniversary of the Six-Day War.

Predictably, an Arab terrorist heaved a grenade at our touring bus. Some of the windows in the rear were shattered but, thanks to God, no one was even scratched. In a confused, semi-panicky state, I considered cancelling the tour for that day and heading back to the relative safety of our hotel. I could just picture the teens calling their parents and begging to let them come home.

My fears were based on a gross misunderstanding of the adolescent psyche. Those teens were too busy picking up particles of broken glass for souvenirs and digging pieces of the grenade out of the back tires for mementos of the trip to be anxious about an errant missile or two.

"Man, was that neat!" they shouted to each other.

"I'll bet no other tour group had that on their itinerary!" (It was hard for me not to take credit for scheduling the episode.)

"Just think, you guys! We were almost martyrs—just like Jesus and the disciples!"

God gives teenagers feet "like a mountain goat" because He wants them to live on "high places" where their faith grows best. He knows that Christian teens thrive in the rarified atmosphere of active mission in the real world.

Our concept of adolescence as a "waiting period" reflects our own failure as parents to comprehend or serve the needs of our teens. By denying the church-related adolescent an immediate role in the church, we prolong his dependence, dismantle his self-esteem, and cripple his capacity to care for others.

Is it any wonder that so many teens feel alienated from religion and unwanted by the church? Should we be surprised when we invoke their cynicism by giving them a perfunctory slap on the back and assuring them that we need them in the church? They know better.

CHRISTIAN TEENS: THE CHURCH OF TODAY

We have unintentionally cultivated at least three heresies by not preparing our teenagers for service in the church.

HERESY # 1: Teenagers are not able to be effective disciples.

I read an interesting article in a psychological journal. The author claimed that the ability to function responsibly and make a solid contribution to the community requires a level of cognitive development and a self-awareness that seldom appear in adolescence. It's a good thing that David didn't read that report until after he introduced Goliath to his Creator, or that John Mark didn't subscribe to that journal before he left on his missionary journey with the Apostle Paul.

The truth is, historically, that when given the chance,

teens have responded valiantly and with profound effect to Christ's command to go "into all the world and make disciples." No one can reach teenagers like teenagers can. Consider the following letter that I received from a high school senior.

Dear Bob,

How's it going? I'm doing great. I just wanted to thank you for being tough on me at camp. I shouldn't have gotten so mad at that softball game. I've always had a pride problem, and you know how I hate to lose. But this time, I've really been different since I rededicated my life to God.

Remember how I told you that I always fell away from God when I got home from camp, and my buddies wanted me to "party" with them again? Well, not this time. God and I decided that my senior year was going to be different. This year, I promised Him that I would stand up for Jesus at school and let Him do whatever He wanted to with me.

Well, guess what? I was elected co-captain of the football team, and I decided to start a Bible study for the players! We meet on Mondays, Wednesdays, and Fridays before school. At first I thought none of the guys would come, and then I figured the guys who did come would mock me out.

I guess I was really shocked when they acted interested. I was even more surprised, but excited, when a bunch of the older guys wanted to become Christians and join my church. God's something else, huh, man?

We had twenty-eight players at our last team Bible study. Not all of them are Christians yet, but when we seniors get done with them, they will be!

Keep praying for me!

Your buddy,
Eric

I heard a poem once that reminds me of Eric's adventure with his high school football team. It may not be sophisticated poetry, but it makes its point.

One teen awake can waken another.
The second can waken his next door's brother.
Three teens awake can rouse the town and
Turn the whole place upside down.
Four teens awake can cause such a fuss
They'll finally awaken the rest of us.

HERESY # 2: *It is enough for the church to keep teenagers busy and "off the streets." To expect any ministry from them is unrealistic and self-deluding.*

A few years ago I worked with a church which honestly faced the fact that its youth program was anemic and badly in need of rejuvenation. After much prayer and discussion, the congregation decided to call as youth minister a dynamic young man who exuded enthusiasm. He was a walking "Youth Activities Ideas Notebook," with a propensity for pizza and an aversion for sleep.

His arrival could have been measured on the Richter scale, as he hit the ground running at full speed. He hustled the teens from the roller skating rink to the swimming pool, from the amusement park to the sand dunes, from the waterslide to the miniature golf course, and regularly scheduled all night "lock-ins" in the church basement. (Is it any wonder that the mortality rate for youth pastors is so high? They either have to move on or die of old age in their early twenties.)

This particular young man finished his first year and was tempted to give himself high marks for what appeared to be a flourishing youth program. His own integrity led him to a different conclusion. Whereas, when he came to the church, he was confronted with approximately a dozen biblically illiterate, spiritually apathetic teens, a year later, he realized that all his work had only quadrupled the problem. Now he had over fifty lukewarm teens suffering from what he called "pew-monia," who had to be entertained and indulged to ensure their attendance.

He resolved to spend less time in his ideas notebook and more in the Bible. Asking God to give the youth group a new focus, he finally made the decision to take the teens on a mission trip to Arizona. He recruited adult sponsors from the congregation, and together they prepared Bible studies to reach Navajo children on an Indian reservation with vacation Bible school. They planned to use the teenagers whenever possible, but the major responsibility for doing ministry rested squarely with the adults.

By the time they arrived at the reservation, the youth pastor and the other chaperones had been driven to distraction by the constant bickering and infighting among the teens on the bus. In fact, they were so frustrated, he felt compelled to make a difficult announcement.

"Tomorrow morning, when the Navajo children arrive at the church, they will not see me or any other adult. If those kids are going to hear about Jesus Christ this week, they will have to hear about Him from you. We refuse to be your baby-sitters. If God is going to do anything, He'll have to do it through you, because we quit."

Even if his decision was an afterthought, born out of frustration, it could not have been more timely or penetrating for that youth group. Natural leaders emerged that evening from among the teens. They planned their own messages and strategies for sharing Christ's love with the Indian children. Not only were the Navajo affected for eternity, but the youth group grew more in two weeks of mission than they had during the previous year of frenetic youth activities.

HERESY # 3: Teenagers are the "church of tomorrow."

No matter how worthy your motive, I encourage you never to give your teenagers that standard lecture about their "potential," especially after you feel they have failed you in some way. Focusing on what you hope they will *become* can make teens feel that they are sorry losers today.

It's only normal for us to have goals for our teenagers, but we must never assume that our dreams for them are also God's purpose. In fact, the goal that seems all important to us as parents might be merely incidental to God. What we see as the process, He sees as the end.

In *My Utmost for His Highest*, Oswald Chambers insightfully reminds us that "God's training is for now, not presently. His purpose is for this minute, not for something in the future. . . . What men call training and preparation, God calls the end."[3]

God's purpose for us and our teens is that we depend on Him and His power today. Adolescents may not fully be who they are going to be, but they are who they are right now. It is this process of being who they are, and not the end result, that is glorifying to God.

There is great hope if we parents and church members recognize that we need our teenagers—not just as the adults that they will be tomorrow, but as the spirited Christians they can be today. Both the church and the home can tap into that spirit by giving teens the chance to participate *while* they are growing.

How will you respond to God's cry, "Let my young people go!"?

CHAPTER
4

What's Hot and What's Not

Reason #2: Negative influence of the media

"AIN'T NOTHING I'D RATHER DO, GOING DOWN IT'S PARTY TIME. MY FRIENDS ARE GOING TO BE THERE, TOO. I'M ON THE HIGHWAY TO HELL." —AC/DC ROCK BAND

ARRIVING A FEW HOURS EARLY for a youth rally in Ohio, I staked out a secluded corner of the choir loft and began to prepare myself for the evening message. After a while, I noticed a teenage girl slip into the auditorium, look around for a moment, and, not seeing me, walk up to the baby grand piano on the stage. She put that Yamaha through its paces with a stirring rendition of "How Great Thou Art." Figuring that she was practicing for the rally, I made no attempt to interrupt. I closed my eyes, leaned back, and prepared to enjoy the "mini-concert."

Her next song was beautiful, and her touch was such that it moved me, though I had never heard the song before. She followed with another familiar church hymn, but repeated the haunting "mystery tune" again. This pattern continued for over half an hour, when she concluded with a delicate interpretation of "Jesus Loves Me, This I Know." As she rose to leave I spoke up.

"Excuse me."

She turned in surprise.

"You play very well, and I just wanted to thank you for inspiring me this afternoon."

She politely replied, "You're welcome," adding, "I didn't know anyone was sitting back there."

"I'm getting a message ready for the rally tonight. I'm going to be challenging the teens to really get involved in the ministry of the church, and you've been a great example. By the way, I recognized everything except for that one beautiful song that you played over and over. What was it?"

"Oh, that. You probably wouldn't know that song."

"Why not?" I asked, thinking she would inform me that it was a brand new gospel hit.

"Because it's the theme song from the 'The Young and the Restless.' "

"That's an old Billy Graham movie, isn't it?" (Whoops! I was thinking of *The Restless Ones!*)

She laughed and sheepishly straightened me out. "No, it's a soap opera on TV. You know, 'The Young and the Restless.' "

The double irony of her song selections was not lost on me. First, the title, "The Young and the Restless," aptly describes many of our church-related teenagers. There is a tendency for us to think of adolescents as too young to be trusted with or trained for significant roles in the church. Their restlessness with the church and its claims on their time and allegiance often results in their departure from the faith.

Secondly, the constant interplay between church hymns and that soap opera tune illustrated for me the constant battle for the full attention of American teenagers. They are caught between the alluring sirens of a soap-opera society and the beckoning voice of Jesus Christ. The world means to have our teens and is making its play for them through the media.

TEENS ON TUNES AND TV

The average responses of the 400 church-related teens in this study to items which measured media influence on their faith were as follows:

"I usually know most of the top ten rock songs." (strongly agree)

"I enjoy watching MTV." (strongly agree)

"Christians should listen only to Christian music." (disagree)

"I'd rather watch TV than read a book." (strongly agree)

"I watch too much TV." (strongly agree)

"I think it's all right for a Christian to go to an R-rated movie." (agree)

"I regularly watch Christian television programming." (strongly disagree)

Our teens are enormously influenced by what they see, hear, and read. In every analysis of the data gathered from the randomly selected students in this study, negative media influence surfaced as the number two predictor of adolescent alienation from religion.

WHO IS IN CONTROL?

Defining secular humanism as "a philosophy which holds that God is nonexistent or irrelevant to human affairs" and that man is "the measure of all things," Franky Schaeffer describes the message with which the media is constantly bombarding today's adolescents. Schaeffer claims that members of the media can be characterized as "liberal" and "humanistic" in such overwhelming numbers that our sources of information have become "utterly biased." He cites Lichter and Rothman's study of 240 journalists and broadcasters which showed that:

In a nation in which seven out of ten Americans say they are church members and sixty percent claim that their religious beliefs are very important, fifty percent of those surveyed had no religious affiliation, and eighty-six percent seldom or never attend religious services.[1]

From the variegated media blitz, our teenagers receive regular input that is diametrically opposed to a Christian world view and consistently at odds with parental preferences. From their survey among media figures, Lichter and Rothman stated,

In their attitudes toward sex and sex roles, members of the media elite are virtually unanimous in opposing the constraints of both government and tradition. . . . Ninety percent agree that a woman has the right to decide for herself whether to have an abortion. Seventy-nine percent agree strongly with this pro-choice position. . . . Fifty-four percent do not regard adultery as wrong, and only fifteen percent strongly agree that extramarital affairs are immoral.[2]

Through the mass media, the church-related teenagers will, for the most part, view the world without Christian coordinates. Often, their ethical supports are knocked from beneath them as questions of right and wrong become relative and Christian absolutes via Biblical authority are nonexistent.

In the same regard, when the media speak of freedom, they usually do so in material or political terms, displaying abject ignorance of Jesus Christ's offer to liberate teenagers from the dominions of self and sin. There is normally a profound silence in the secular media about the positive value of Christianity. When the subject of religion is dealt with at all, it is usually denigrated or ridiculed. Schaeffer quotes part of an article entitled "TV Preachers Stoke the Hell Fires" to illustrate a typical presentation of Christian authority by the media:

*All over America, at all hours of the day, the TV
preachers are spewing their "Christian" messages about
God and the devil. . . . The preachers are respected
citizens; presidents take their calls; lesser politicians
and network executives fear them; the tax laws make
them rich. But they specialize in one thing—the
peddling of fear. Fear of "secular humanism,"
Communism, big government, labor unions,
liberalism, other Americans, all mixed up with fear of
the Lord and fear of Satan. We know their true
enemies: reason, intelligence, pluralism.* [3]

THE TV EXPERIENCE

The three main sources of adult influence which shaped
the lives of teenagers for centuries were the church, the
home, and the school. These have been eclipsed in the
present generation by the single greatest molding influence:
television.[4]

There are "watchdog" groups of parents and politicians
locked in daily battle with the Federal Communications
Commission over the content of television programming.
The major focuses of the controversy are sex and violence,
and the stakes are high. But, along with the content, I am at
least as concerned with the actual experience of watching
TV. George Will writes in the *Washington Post:*

*The principal worry is not that repeated exposure to
depictions of cruelty will make persons act cruelly.
Rather, it is that it will produce persons who can
respond only to depictions of excess. A generation raised
on "slash films" (like Halloween, Friday the 13th, etc.)
may become unable to enjoy subtlety, nuance, or
delicacy.* [5]

The average Christian seventeen-year-old has watched
over 18,000 hours of TV while spending only a few hours a
week at church. As our teens continue to indiscriminately tune
in, George Will warns us that we can expect them to become

less sensitive, less involved, less civilized—in a word, less.

I remain troubled by the negative effects which so much television viewing must have upon the teenager's struggle to grow in the Christian faith. Several factors should be considered.

1. Television viewing prepares the teen to expect quick and easy answers to his problems, as nightly he observes crises being solved in thirty or sixty minutes. The adolescent who is conditioned by TV's "quick-fix syndrome" often finds genuine problem-solving skills beyond his reach. But more important ultimately is his view of Christianity, which not only offers no magical formulas or cheap panaceas, but encourages responsible perseverance and warns that suffering is often a part of God's program.

2. It is a fact that teenagers of the television generation have been conditioned by intense sensory stimulation of the right hemisphere of the brain (more sensual and emotional) to the deprivation of developing the brain's left hemisphere (more rational and evaluative). Thus television simply reinforces the teenager's tendency to be dominated by his feelings rather than his reason.

I doubt if I'm the only parent who has heard his teen say, "I don't know why I did it, Dad. I just felt like it, that's all." Or, "It was an impulse. I guess I should have thought it through first, huh?" Or maybe, "It just felt so good, I got swept away by the whole thing. I didn't have time to think about the consequences."

Let's face it: I have three daughters, and there is an excellent chance that most of the boys who will be interested in them will have a poorly developed left hemisphere function. From a lifetime of being baby-sat by the TV and having their thinking and communicating done for them, they will approach their dates with one of my girls with a heavy reliance on nonverbal, sensory experiences and Neanderthal communicative skills. (Do you think I'm being too hard? Just wait till your daughters reach dating age!)

When your children reach adolescence, with all of its tensions, transitions, and temptations, they will need the ability to think for themselves and make tough, clear-headed decisions. It is not too difficult to understand how teenagers who have been conditioned to expect immediate gratification and whose prime motivator is pleasure might opt for the escapism of drugs, sex, and alcohol while rejecting the reality that Christianity challenges them to confront.

3. The pace and technology of television train teenagers to passively encode what they are viewing without carefully evaluating it. When the teen's mind is in a beta wave pattern, he is analyzing what he is watching. But Dr. Richard Fredericks reports that when viewing TV, the minds of most teenagers are in an alpha wave pattern. This means that their minds are usually reduced to a state of passivity (non-analytical) and are highly susceptible to incoming ideas. The problem is that as these concepts are passively encoded with no discrimination, they are stored and later affect the adolescent's choices and behavior.[6]

SO, WHAT'S A PARENT TO DO? PART I

Pausing outside the sanctuary of a church, I noticed the banner festively announcing the theme of the special meetings. "Family Emphasis Week!" it shouted in capital letters, "Come Every Night!!!" Then, in smaller type, it advised, "Help Pack a Pew. Bring a Friend."

I couldn't help but envision how Jesus, who made a decided nuisance of Himself by relentlessly pushing his hearers to deal with causes instead of effects, might have rewritten the message on that banner: "Family Emphasis Week. Stay Home Every Night!!! Turn Your TV Off. Become Friends." (After all, this is the man who said, "If your right eye causes you to sin, pluck it out.")

Richard Fredericks reports that over thirty percent of our

homes today are classified as "constant television families," meaning that the TV is never turned off during the day, even when no one is watching it. Television is becoming the babbling backdrop against which our whole lives are being played out.[7]

Seldom do I visit a Christian home where the television is not the focal point of the household, reigning over whatever room the family spends most of its time in. Scheduled to speak in the New England area, I was excited to find that I would be staying at the home of a family I had grown very close to during my college days. With my anticipation building from the airport to their home, you can imagine my letdown when I burst into their living room, only to be greeted with, "Shhh! Be quiet! This is the best part!"

It was not a put-down to me personally—they hadn't even looked up to see who the intruder was. The President of the United States would have fared no better. I stood there silently and observed three generations, the mother, daughter, and grandmother, transfixed by a soap-opera drama in the middle of the afternoon. We had a good laugh about my "welcome," and I treasure their friendship no less, but the lesson of television's encroachment into our daily lives was not lost on me.

Subtly, television has usurped a position of influence that no Christian family ever meant for it to have. Would it not make more sense for us to treat it as any other appliance we invite into our homes?

We do not leave the lawn mower in the middle of the yard when we are finished with it; we put it away. We do not leave the vacuum turned on in the corner after we have cleaned the carpet; we turn it off and put it back in the closet where it belongs. We could begin to fumigate the airwaves of our homes by finding a place to put away the television set when we are done with it, bringing it out again only for special occasions.

If that isn't radical enough, consider life without television.

"We went through a few days of real withdrawal when the TV broke down, especially knowing that we didn't have enough money to get it fixed that month. As I look back on it now, that was one of the best months our family ever had."

We've all heard testimonies like this one. Yes, life goes on without television, and for some families, it would be much richer.

A few years ago, my wife and one of her friends went into Chicago to be a part of the audience for a Phil Donahue special entitled, "The Influence of Television on the Home." Donahue introduced his guest experts and, after baiting them with controversial questions, turned them loose to sell the viewers their opinions.

Partway through the show, one of the guests turned to the studio audience and remarked, "Of course, each of you has two or three TV sets at home."

At that point, Donahue interrupted. "There's no one out there who doesn't have a television, is there?"

My wife looked around and saw no response. She confided later, "I saw my own arm going up and I wondered, 'What am I getting myself into?'"

In disbelief, Donahue leaped to his feet and scaled the steps to the row in which Joyce was sitting. She slowly rose and tried to ready herself for the onslaught that she knew was coming.

Incredulity characterized his part of the ensuing interview. "Are you kidding me, lady? You live in America and don't own a television set?"

"No, we don't, and haven't had one for over five years."

"But how do you survive? What do you do? Do you have children? What do they think about it?"

"We are Christians," my wife calmly replied, "and family is very important to us. We were concerned that television was stealing too much from us, so we decided as a family to get rid of it. I really don't believe that our children miss it at all. They're too busy. We read books around the fireplace, work puzzles together, play board games, and are so heavily involved with all kinds of sports that there is no time to miss television."

Donahue maintained his skepticism and continued to treat her as an anachronism; a throwback to the Neanderthal housewife. But Joyce held her ground, defending our decision by pointing to the results: self-actualized children who are good students because they have incentive to read, and a family whose members are in true relationship with one another.

Donahue finally announced that the show would break for a commercial. Then he took my wife over to the side of the auditorium and said two last things to her.

"Okay, now you can tell me the truth. You really do have a TV, don't you—even a little one in the closet or something, huh?"

After she repeated that such was not the case, he scratched his head and ended their conversation with, "Lady, I'm going to make sure that we get your name and address. I don't think there is anybody else like you, and we may need you to come back on this show."

The truth is, of course, that there are many others like us. There are parents all over this country who care about the formation of their children's character and the spiritual milieu of their homes.

There's another invasion alarming these concerned parents, and that is the movies that, thanks to the VCR, can come right into our homes. Parents of teens should carefully select the films they attend and the video cassettes they bring home.

Young minds are like sponges. They need to be careful about what puddle they are sitting in.

Many years ago my wife and I double-dated with a

couple from the seminary I was attending. It was a beautiful summer evening, so we decided on a drive-in that was showing *True Grit,* an academy award winner for John Wayne. We paid no attention to what was showing on the opposite screen of the outdoor cinema until a theater attendant waved his flashlight at our approaching car.

"Sorry, pal," he yelled. "This side is filled up. You can either go back and get a refund or watch the other movie."

No contest. We pulled into the adjacent lot, stocked up on buttered popcorn and soft drinks, and settled in to enjoy a movie we knew nothing about.

That was over fifteen years ago, and I can still remember the title that scrolled across the screen: *A Weekend with the Baby-Sitter.* There has been more than one occasion in the past few decades when I wished that the title was all I could remember about the ten minutes that we watched.

When Jesus said, "The eye is the lamp of the body," He knew of what He spoke. Even unintentional voyeurism at the movies can leave indelible impressions on a mind that is sure to be barraged with as much illicit sexual pressure as the Christian psyche can withstand.

It would be the better part of wisdom to find credible sources for movie reviews and pay attention to them. Several Christian magazines now contain helpful reviews for alert parents and discerning teens. *Campus Life,* in particular, has an excellent monthly media guide geared to the Christian teenager.

Don't put too much faith in the movie industry's rating system. Have you ever rented a video cassette movie for your family, only to find out in the inner sanctum of your own living room that the expert who rated it must have been comatose during his viewing?

Let's settle it once and for all: PG no longer guarantees an innocuous cinematic adventure. In fact, it often seems to stand for "Pretty Gross." So, rather than set boundaries within which your teens can indiscriminately watch whatever they want (e.g., G for your grade schoolers, PG for your junior-highers, PG-13 for your high-schoolers, and R for any children who are still living at home when they are over 100 years of age), it would be wiser to develop trustworthy sources among your church friends and like-minded neighbors to keep you and your teens informed about movies to steer away from and those to watch.

"Happy is the parent or teen who does not watch in the counsel of the ungodly."

JESUS IS THE ROCK AND HE'LL ROLL YOUR BLUES AWAY

We are in a battle, and the field on which it is being contended is the mind of your teenager. Having little success in their first few years in the rock scene, Mick Jagger and the Rolling Stones devised a formula which was to vault them to the top of the music charts. Jagger publicly warned, "From now on, we're going after the mind."[8] This rock group has effectively been seducing the minds of adolescents for over twenty years, serving as models for scores of other groups who have copied or extended their perverted sexual and satanic themes.

A brief survey may be enlightening for many parents.

BOY GEORGE ANNOUNCES, *"I don't believe in God, that there's somebody up there with a bowl of rice waiting to feed us. I believe in life after death; I think we all end up as maggots and that sort of thing. After all, we fertilize the earth, don't we?"[9]*

STEVE SMITH OF JOURNEY SAYS, *"Rock stars are known for how many women they can take home or how much drugs they can consume."[10]*

PETER CHRIS OF KISS CLAIMS, *"I find myself evil. I believe in the devil as much as God. You can use either to get things done."[11]*

PRINCE, A TEEN IDOL WHOSE ALBUM "DIRTY MIND"
SETS A NEW STANDARD FOR SEXUAL PERVERSION,
BOASTS THAT, *Incest is everything it is said to be.*[12]

I have yet to meet the teenager who could effectively live
as a Christian while being bludgeoned with the unrelenting
message of secular rock music. Granted, there are some non-
issues over which we parents waste much time and energy,
but secular rock music and its negative influence on the
mind and life of your teens is not one of them. Make no
mistake about it, your teenagers' perception of the Christian
faith, their relationship with you, indeed, the entirety of their
world view will be enormously affected by the kind of music
that grips their imagination.

I prayed with a teenage girl at a youth convention about
the struggle she was having to stay sexually pure. She related
that she came from a Christian home, but no matter how hard
she tried to be God's girl in her dating life, she inevitably
wound up with the wrong kind of guy who would misuse her
sexually. Maybe I just played a hunch, or perhaps I've learned
something about teens and what misshapes them, but I asked
her a question which surely seemed unrelated to her. "By the
way, what kind of music do you listen to?" She gave me a
puzzled look and wondered aloud what her music had to do
with her problem.

I suggested that a man named Solomon might have a clue
for her. Long before behavioral scientists began to document
the observable phenomenon that you become what you think
about, God spoke through a wise king: "As a man thinks in
his heart, so is he" (Proverbs 23:7a). I added that the New
Testament advises, "Fix your thoughts on things that are
good, and true, and right" (Philippians 4:8, LB).

She admitted that she spent a lot of hours listening to
secular rock and that her walls were crowded with posters of
rock stars. In fact, she confessed, the last thing she saw at
night was a poster of David Lee Roth, lead singer for Van

Halen, chained in a seminude, sadomasochistic position.

Roth publicly blusters, "I'm in the job to exercise my sexual fantasies. When I'm on stage it's like doing it with 20,000 of your closest friends. . . . I'm proud of the way we live."[13]

What chance was this girl giving her own virginity by opening up her thought patterns to the merciless input of voices diametrically opposed to her Christian upbringing?

Toab Hooper, the producer of the grotesque *Texas Chainsaw Massacre,* describes my young friend's dilemma accurately: "Subliminal perception [assimilating ideas which become a part of your psychological makeup without being aware of it] is a killer. The capacity of the unconscious to take information and run with it is unlimited. We flatter ourselves by thinking we're in control of our thinking."[14]

The typical teenager absorbs between three and five hours of rock music every day via MTV, radio, and the home stereo. How long can even a Christian teen hold out under such a steady bombardment of sex, drugs, satanic ritual, and suicide?

After reading a chapter entitled, "Merchants of Death: Touting Teen Suicide" in Tipper Gore's book, I am convinced there is a correlation between the music teens listen to and the escalation of suicide attempts among adolescents.

Gore, wife of Senator Albert Gore and co-founder of the Parents' Music Resource Center, cited a moving letter which she received from the grieving mother of a young male suicide victim. She revealed that her son was only six weeks away from high school graduation in the top five percent of his class. He was accepted by a prestigious college and appeared to have everything going for him. His autopsy exposed no trace of drugs.

The mother wrote: "When my husband and I were going through his papers after he died, we found the words to a rock song, "Suicide Solution." We asked his girlfriend about the words and she told us it was his favorite song. I feel that these words opened up a tragic alternative to him that he would not have otherwise considered. . . ."[15]

Speaking out against the perversity of secular rock music, Mark Kelly of the Christian band, Petra, who carried the casket of a seventeen-year-old friend to its grave following a tragic, drug-induced suicide, challenges, "Who influenced him that suicide was an easy way out? Who is infiltrating the minds of our young generation that gives birth to one new teen drug addict every thirty seconds, one new teen alcoholic every twenty seconds, and one more unwanted teen pregnancy every forty-five seconds? The brainwash is so successful that it is exterminating much of our generation!"[16]

SO, WHAT'S A PARENT TO DO? PART II

First, familiarize yourself with the secular rock scene.

My introduction to MTV (music television) came one afternoon at a small, midwestern Christian college where I had come to lead several hundred teenagers in a Bible study. I walked through the crowded TV lounge of the dormitory on my way to the auditorium. There was tension when I walked into the crowded room and a few of the teens looked up and recognized me as the Bible conference speaker. They looked away quickly, and one got up to leave. The decibel level was shattering as approximately thirty others sat mesmerized by a bizarre group called Twisted Sister screaming out their latest hit, "We're Not Going to Take It Anymore"—a song which encourages teens to rise up against their parents and other authority figures.

I vowed that day to learn enough about secular rock without becoming a part of it to be able to minister to kids who were caught up in it and, I hoped, to bring them back to Christianity. There is a good chance that most parents and even a few youth pastors have very little idea just what their teens are listening to.

Secondly, let teens have their own Christian music.

Larry Norman is right when he sings, "Why Should the Devil Have All the Good Music?" When Martin Luther set solid Christian theology to the barroom tunes of his day (hymns which we now sing with staid decorum in our Sunday morning worship services), he was establishing a precedent for exactly what is happening today in the best of the contemporary Christian music scene.

Carman's "Champion," a moving song about the Resurrection, has inspired thousands of Christian teens to look to the Lord Jesus Christ as their hero and salvation. Steve Camp's latest albums constitute a penetrating challenge to teens to follow Christ into deeper patterns of discipleship. Russ Taff's clarion call to Christian commitment seems to be getting stronger and more effective among youth every year. Bob Hartman of Petra says, "The world doesn't need another secular band. We want to be a band that goes out and boldly proclaims the Gospel of Jesus Christ."[17] The list could go on.

Granted, because contemporary Christian music is big business, and Christian recording artists are still human beings, there are excesses and inconsistencies. But the fact remains that God is doing something wonderful among Christian teens through the influence of committed Christian musicians. I am eternally in the debt of Michael W. Smith, Amy Grant, Sandi Patti, White Heart, Petra, Oasis, and others for the impact they have had on the growing faith of my children. You cannot know my inner joy when I overhear, through the thin plaster of the bedroom walls, one of my teens singing along with Mylon LeFevre's song of uncompromising faith, "Love God, Hate Sin!"

Teenagers are going through that critical phase of life when they need to become their own people. The music which they choose is an important part of that identity, and judicious parents will make it as desirable as possible for their teens to choose contemporary Christian music over secular rock.

Finally, take time to listen to their music with them.

Just because it's their music doesn't mean there can't be special moments when you find them listening in their rooms and sit down to really try and hear what they are hearing. That they know it isn't your kind of music will most likely make them value your effort all the more. The affirmation of your presence will say much to them—not the least being that you care about staying in touch with their world.

CHAPTER 5

The Power of a Parent's Love

Reason #3: Poor relationship with parents

I HAVE A GOOD FRIEND WHO can't remember his father ever telling him that he loved him as a teenager. He worked so hard for so long to win his dad's love. Practicing baseball for hours almost every day of the summer, he hoped that when he stepped up to the plate in a real game, he would make his dad proud of him.

Pitchers love to throw the ball to batters who are concentrating more on impressing their fathers than on a hard-breaking curve ball. He remembers feeling that critical gaze from the bleachers, checking his batting stance, looking for a flaw in his swing.

"Strike three!!" the umpire cried.

My friend walked to the car with his head hung in silence. He knew his father would never mention the nice catch he had made in that same game, or the double he'd hit in the sixth inning to chase home the tying run. All of his attention would be on the strikeout.

Verbally expressing love and motivating by encouragement were simply not the dad's style. He was his son's critic, and the boy feared him. It's ironic; he was convinced that his father didn't like him very much, yet he was obsessed with pleasing him. Getting high marks in school seemed to be the best way of doing that. His goal was to be valedictorian in a graduating class of almost 600, and he pursued that objective with a vengeance.

The day came when he proudly handed the father a report card that boasted straight A's, except for an A-minus in Analytic Geometry. All of his dad's comments were about the "low" grade. Just what was it that the boy could not grasp about the subject? Why had he not done extra credit to bring that grade up?

Was that the day my friend realized that winning his father's love was impossible? Was it then he began not caring what his father thought of him, growing distant, feeding the bitterness which purposed to take control?

Sometime during high school, he made an unconscious decision to be as unlike his father as possible. The dad was austere and emotionally cautious. The son almost reveled in his emotional roller-coaster rides; euphoric one day, despairing the next.

He never saw his father shed a tear. Therefore, there were many nights he would cry himself to sleep listening to maudlin love songs on KXOK radio out of St. Louis.

The father was a Sunday school teacher and sponsor for their church youth group. Accordingly, the son was securely on the road to rejecting Christianity.

THE HIGH COST OF HYPOCRISY

My survey is not the only one to reveal that teenage alienation from religion is highly correlated with a poor relationship between a teen and his parents. The National Sunday School Association administered a poll among 2,000 conservative Protestant parishes. When asked why they had been alienated from the church, the teenagers gave "adult hypocrisy" as their second most frequent reply.[1] Teens are quick to detect duplicity in religion and are uninhibited in using it as a rationale for their own alienation from the church.

In his book, *Psychology of Adolescence,* Dr. Marvin Powell says, "The home environment must be a living example of religious influences in operation and not one that pays mere lip service to religion. Attendance at church on Sunday followed by six days of no trace of religion is not likely to develop a good religious adjustment in the youngster."[2]

Perhaps if there were more genuine home religion, there would be more spiritual power in the church, and our teens would be attracted to the Source of that power.

A number of teens in my own study shared deep concern about the negative effect which parents were having on their relationship with God.

I haven't had the great feeling of being loved by my family. I guess I've been depressed. It's hard to keep faith sometimes when neither one of my parents or step-parents are Christians.

I'm mixed up. It's really hard because I've been a Christian for a little over a year, and my Dad is pretty much set against religion. I stumble a lot and fall.

I hope and pray now that my Mom and Dad will become Christians, too.

I've hit a low point in my life. My parents and I do not get along, and there is much fighting in my home. My parents do not always live as they profess, and that upsets me.

My friends who don't go to church seem more Christian than the members of my church. So I guess I wonder a lot because I see so many people who appear fake.

Moral preaching which is not backed up by consistent

behavior is largely a waste of time. Not only do children do as we do, but many teenagers have a tendency to do as we did, not as we are now saying. I have known more than one family where the parents came to Christ at middle age, only to find their teenagers doggedly determined not to follow them in that decision. It's as if the non-Christian attitudes and behavior patterns they learned from their parents as younger children were so deeply infused that it becomes a formidable task for them to break away from those habitual modes of unbelief when they are capable of making their own decisions as teenagers.

While this phenomenon presents a challenge to parents who wait until their children are teenagers before they decide for Christ, it should also serve as some encouragement for parents who are raising their teens in the church.

Benjamin Keeley measured the religiosity of both Christian and non-Christian high school students. The results of his study showed that teenagers who recognized their parents as deeply committed to their religion were significantly more religious than teens who saw their parents as less committed.[3] The faith (or lack of faith) of the parents has a profound impact upon the faith status of the teenager.

A young pastor in Kansas once told me how his father, a Christian businessman, had wisely made it more likely that his son would stay faithful to God during his decisive teenage years. The father converted what might have seemed an architectural disaster into a steady Christian witness that had eternal ramifications for his children.

Whoever built his home had placed the only downstairs bathroom just off the master bedroom, necessitating frequent trips through that room by the children. The father judiciously planned his daily prayer time during the most highly trafficked period of the evening. The son, who became a pastor, said that he hardly every brushed his teeth without first having to step carefully over his praying father. He recounted that during his teenage years and into college, whenever confronted with temptation, the Holy Spirit would impress upon him a mental picture of his father kneeling by the bed.

The steady devotion of teenagers' parents is crucial to the development of their own faith. "No matter how hard we resist the idea," says Virginia Gibbon, in *PTA Magazine,* "there is no substitute for a parent's moral standards and spiritual values."[4]

SEVEN NOT-SO-EASY, NOT-SO-QUICK STEPS

Adolescent alienation from religion is a complex problem and, as we are finding in this book, there are many different sources of it. Still, we can isolate several key "home factors" which we parents can work on to keep teens from rejecting our Christian values. Here are seven significant strategies that parents can employ to improve relationships with their teens.

1. Renew your own passion for Christ.

"Create in me a clean heart, O God, and renew a right spirit within me . . . Restore to me the joy of your salvation" (Psalm 51: 10, 12a).

One of my professors in graduate school perceptively stated that all of the books on theology in all the dusty archives of all the seminaries in the world pale to insignificance when compared with the influence of one man with a "hallelujah" in his soul. Dead orthodoxy breeds the same. When we look for reasons why our teens are apathetic about their faith, sometimes we need look no further than our own lifeless rituals and barren religious routines.

> *"For that which we are about to receive, we give Thee thanks."*
>
> *"Now I lay me down to sleep, I pray the Lord my soul to keep. . . ."*
>
> *"Bless this food to our bodies, and us to Thy service. . . ."*

59

How many hundreds of times do our teens hear similar "canned" prayers before they write off our religious clichés as insipid drivel and a waste of their time? Whether they call themselves Christians or not, teenagers have an innate sense that God doesn't require archaic invocations to make contact with Him, and doesn't appreciate wearisome patterns of worship anymore than they do.

Often when counseling a troubled teen, I will ask, "Are your parents Christians?" I have wondered what it would mean to parents if they could hear their child reply, "No, not really. They go to church, but it doesn't make any difference."

Ask God to bring vitality and spontaneity back to your own faith. The religious sincerity and enthusiasm of the parents is an important factor in influencing the faith of a teen.

2. *Verbally express your love for your teenager.*

"Be imitators of God, therefore, as dearly loved children, and live a life of love." (Ephesians 5:1, 2a)

There is one thing you can give your teens that they can get from no other source in the cosmos: a parent's love.

From their research with adolescents, Peck and Havighurst say, "The major determinants of character in the parent-child interaction appear to be love and discipline."[5]

I have carried in my briefcase for over ten years a remarkable letter from a high school girl with two common requests. She wrote,

> *Home is getting to be the place I least like to be. It seems that we fight more than anything else, especially me and my Dad. He has never told me that he loves me, and from the way we've been getting along this year, I really don't think he does. Please pray for us.*

As soon as I read those words, I began praying for her father to tell her and show her that he loved her. Then she made her second request.

And there's one more thing. Please pray for me to stay a virgin. When I get married someday, I want to give my husband the gift of my virginity. But I'm dating a non-Christian boy [a common error in judgment made by many Christian girls with non-Christian fathers], *and he's putting a lot of pressure on me to have sex.*

It was an emotional experience for me to turn the page and read the words she wrote the next day to finish her letter.

It's okay, Bob. You don't have to pray for me anymore. I went out on a date with my boyfriend last night. We were in the car and he said, "You're really beautiful." I knew what he wanted, but I wasn't going to give it to him. Then he said the magic words, "I love you," and I melted. I gave him what he asked for.

Her experience was almost too predictable.

3. Keep their confidences and take them seriously.

"He who goes about as a tale-bearer reveals secrets, but he who is trustworthy conceals a matter" (Proverbs 11:13).

One character trait that is essential for developing a strong friendship with anyone is the ability to be confidential. Friends seal a special intimacy by sharing things with each other which they want only a few selected people to know.

There are some people who would have us believe that teenagers will not divulge their private lives to their parents, and that even if they did, because of their limited experience, they would share nothing of consequence. Neither notion has any merit. The truth is that if teens know they will be taken seriously and that whatever they reveal will be trustingly guarded, most of them would welcome a good friend for a parent.

They are wise parents who do not make light of those matters which their teenagers consider important. Whether the problem is a low test grade, a heart-breaking experience with Cupid, or a run-away complexion, if it matters to our teens, then it should matter to us. Privileged is the mother or father who is trusted as a sounding board and confidante.

4. *Be vulnerable, and admit it when you're wrong.*

"Admit your faults to one another and pray for each other so that you may be healed" (James 5:16a, LB).

There are three seldom-heard phrases that, if spoken genuinely, could breach a growing gap between teens and their parents: "I'm sorry." "I was wrong." "Please forgive me."

Sometime between noticing the opposite sex and signing up for driver's training, most teenagers discover that their parents are fallible human beings. Not only do they start beating us at Monopoly and Scrabble, but often they surpass us in the game of honesty, morality, and conscience.

The problem lies not in their accurate perception of our imperfections but in our stubborn refusal to admit it. Not accustomed to having our counsel questioned or motives critiqued, many of us become defensive, garrisoning ourselves against criticism and self-exposure. Such a tactic will only further distance us from our teens.

Being vulnerable and confessing your humanity can have two positive effects upon your relationship with your teenager.

First, your show of vulnerability makes you a touchable person. It is almost impossible to feel close to someone who insists on always being right.

When my children were younger, we used to read books about "The Berenstain Bears." The papa bear was the same in every story, a lovable, bumbling, know-it-all with a knack for sticking his nose into a honeycomb with all the angry bees in the woods still at home.

Once we were reading an episode where the old bear dragged his hapless family from one picnic spot to another, only to have each choice meet with a minor disaster. Suddenly one of my children yelled out, "Hey, Dad! You're just like Papa Berenstain! He messes up just like you do!"

Of course, this observation met with applause from the rest of the kids and approval from my wife. What could I say? They were right, and the nickname has stuck. My family has not only kept me humble three or four times—all right! Hundreds of times!—with the moniker "Papa Berenstain," but I know that God has used it to endear my teenagers to me and keep me touchable.

Secondly, exposing your weaknesses can do much to prepare your teens to face with some resiliency their adolescent years, which are often characterized by anxiety and discouragement over failures.

A teenager whom I've appreciated for years because of his tender heart and sensitivity to others recently came to my office in despair. He and some of his buddies had been arrested for "TP-ing" (draping with toilet paper) an entire neighborhood in the small town where he lived. He suffered the humiliation of having to call his well-known parents to come and sign his release from the police station.

"I just want to run away," he lamented. "My Dad is right. I'm no good. I don't belong in my family. Everybody in it is perfect except for me!"

How that young man needed to hear his father receive him graciously and confess some of the fading blunders of his own adolescence.

5. *Never embarrass your teenager.*

"And if your brother sins, go and reprove him in private" (Matthew 18:15a, NAS).

The occasion was an open house for Tim's high school graduation. I was sitting with the rest of the guests in a spacious living room, listening to a story that his father was telling about him.

"Yes, sir, his mother and I wonder how Tim is even

going to survive when he gets out on his own at college. That boy can't walk and chew gum at the same time. Why, do you know what he did last week? It's hard to believe that anyone with a high school education could. . . . "

I watched the new graduate flush crimson while his father proceeded to recite a worthless story which made his own son out to be an idiot. (Personally, I had my own opinion as to which person at the reception should have been tested for intelligence). Almost everyone laughed at the father's anecdote. Even Tim managed a good-natured smile, but his body language betrayed his inner humiliation.

The point is that Tim's father had an opportune moment to create a warm memory for his son. Instead, he alienated his teen and gave him another reason not to write home from college.

6. *Forgive and forget.*

"Love keeps no record of wrongs" (I Corinthians 13:5).

Through mutual friends, I recently was introduced to a large, gray-haired man in his late fifties.

"I'm Bill Stanner," he said, reaching out a massive hand to greet me.

His voice was rich and resonant, and I took an immediate liking to my new acquaintance.

"Stanner," I mused. "I went to college with a beautiful girl whose last name was Stanner. Jessica Stanner. Are you related?"

There was an instant transformation in his expression. The ready smile disappeared, his face hardened into a mask of austerity.

I'd unintentionally struck a sensitive chord in this man's heart which must have caused painful memories to wash back over him.

He looked down and said, "She was my daughter."

Not knowing what to say, I stuttered, "I'm sorry, Mr.

Stanner. I didn't know. I hadn't heard."

"Heard what?" came his brusque reply. "That she's dead? She didn't die! I'm not that lucky. I just don't claim her anymore."

Sensing that he expected a response, I offered, "Do you want to talk about it?"

"There's nothing to talk about." He paused, probably wavering between opening up or getting up—and leaving. He started in again, speaking in clipped sentences, his anger building.

"I don't know what more I could have done for her! You have no idea. I gave her everything she asked for. I trusted her, and she lied to me. She's just no good, that's all."

It was obvious to me that he still loved his daughter. He could not have been as ravaged by whatever it was she did, unless he had made a deep and irrevocable emotional investment in her.

I hurt for this man and his daughter, and wondered if it would be presumptuous of me to ask him about the possibility of forgiving her.

As if he could read my mind, he closed our conversation with, "Don't think I haven't tried to forgive her. I tried that a lot of times. But I could never forget what she did."

Can we truly say that we have made an honest attempt to forgive our teens if we have not purposed to put their offenses behind us? A refusal to forgive and forget has turned more than one parent's bed into a sleepless rack of torture, and more than one home into a tense, acrimonious battlefield to play out the parent-teen years.

In Hebrews 8:12, God Himself says, "and I will remember their sins no more." If the Infinite Memory can erase all records of our sins against Him, surely He can lead us toward a wholesome amnesia regarding the wrongdoings of our teens.

Giving your teens room to fail will pay great dividends

for building your relationship with them. The path of wisdom for a parent is to decide early on that there are no unforgivable, nor unforgettable teenage sins.

7. *Give your teenager your time.*

". . . redeeming the time, for the days are evil" (Ephesians 5:16).

There are a number of excellent books on Christian parenting, and many of them deal extensively with the issues of setting priorities and budgeting time for your family. Although most of these authors point us in the right direction, I have yet to read one who I felt challenged me to go far enough.

Perhaps knowing only too well the tyrannical grasp that the hour hand has on our families, many counselors advise us to spend "quality time" with our adolescents. I had almost bought into that approach, until I had an unsettling experience that caused me to rethink.

I'd been on the road for over three weeks and was speaking in the final city on my itinerary. My responsibility in that last series of meetings was to preach on the weeknights and encourage the crowd to invite as many people as possible to return and hear a well-known evangelist speak on the weekend.

My own level of anticipation rose daily until Friday evening finally arrived. The auditorium was packed with people who had faithfully responded to my nightly challenge to return with friends to hear this highly respected personality. I felt gratified and "fully wired" to tune into his message.

I watched the man take his place in the pulpit, my pen poised to take copious notes. As it turned out, the only thing I wrote down was his opening text.

Sitting in the front row, I was probably one of the first to notice that something was wrong. He stared down at his notes, as curiosity and tension grew in the crowd. When he faced the audience again, deep emotion etched his face. Then with deliberation he made an unsettling announcement.

"I—I'm really sorry," he stammered, "but I cannot speak tonight."

My body went rigid. *What!?* I thought. *You've got to talk! That's why we're all here. This huge crowd has come just to hear your message.*

The tears in the speaker's eyes were enough to silence my objections. Then came the few words that were to constitute that evening's sermon.

"I don't know what to say. Last night in Nevada, my twenty-eight-year-old son took me aside and said, 'Dad, I know that God has used you in great crusades all over the world, and that's why you weren't around much when I was growing up. But, Dad, I've got to tell you this, and I know it's going to hurt you. I don't even know who you are.'"

The speaker slowly scanned the crowd, as if searching for someone who could understand why he had to finish and leave.

"If you can help it," he concluded, "you must never put one of your children in a situation where he will have to say to you what my son said to me last night."

I felt I could not breathe. Though many around me were sobbing, and the altar before me was beginning to fill, I knew that his words were for me. That eloquent one-minute message redirected my attention from my vocation to my family. I vowed to God that, with His help, each of my children would learn to know me well, even if they took for granted having me around home.

And so, while others are advising parents to spend "quality time" with their families, if only in small increments, I am of a mind that even that may not be enough. I know that I run the risk of not being heard on this subject, because I am asking for more than most parents feel they are able to give. But I honestly believe that teens take time, even if on the surface they act like they'd rather not be in the same galaxy with their parents.

It seems to me that when we choose to have children, we make another choice that is easily forgotten in this day of upward mobility: we choose to spend time with them. Few experts dispute that infants and younger children need constant care and focused attention. Just because the character of a child is largely formed by the time he leaves elementary school, we should not presume that our influence or responsibility as parents is diminished. On the contrary, there are whole new dimensions that can evolve when building a friendship with a teen. And friendships take time—"quality time" and then some.

A stranger asked me recently what my vocation was. Before I could answer with my salaried position and say, "I teach Bible at a Christian college," one of my neurons misfired and the truth came out. "I'm a taxi cab driver for my teenagers."

After driving them to and picking them up from karate, ballet, art, swimming, piano, and horseback riding, wrestling, volleyball, baseball, football, and basketball, whatever else you do in life is strictly a sideline. But these many and varied blocks of time that you spend with your teens in the mundane, daily give-and-take of life are crucial for your relationship with them.

It is while driving together, or fishing down on the riverbank, or rebuilding a car engine in the garage, that the bridge is firmly constructed to span the generation gap and provide your teen with a father or mother who is also a good friend and a willing listener.

Besides, those invaluable teachable moments seldom choose the same "quality time" frames that we painstakingly set aside for them. I spent weeks planning for and praying about a long overdue "facts of life" conversation with my son. My wife promised me that she would discuss sex with our daughters when they were older, if I would explain the topic to my son. Even though I had some anxiety about it, I wanted my thirteen-year-old to learn in a Christ-centered way from me what I had picked up piecemeal fashion from lewd jokes and loose sexual banter when I was his age.

Setting aside a weekend in August, I decided to surround our man-to-man talk with enough entertainment to keep his enthusiasm level high and give me time to mentally rehearse my speech. For starters, we attended a Chicago White Sox baseball game and then headed for a camping excursion at Indiana Beach. We spent most of Saturday swimming in the lake and sunbathing on the pier, reading aloud Jim Dobson's book, *Preparing for Adolescence.*

After incinerating a few hot dogs over the campfire that evening, I knew that the time had arrived. I turned to face my boy, screwed up my courage, took a deep breath, and said—"Would you like to play some miniature golf right now?"

"You bet! Let's go!" he cried, and I wiped the perspiration from my forehead.

Later that evening, I remembered my duty, and as we lay in our sleeping bags by the campfire, we looked up at the stars and I talked to him about sex. About a half an hour later, with the coals in the fire glowing red, I finished my torturous explanation and asked, "Well, what do you think, pal?"

I could feel my heart pounding. Did he understand what I'd said? Had I been too technical? Or was he simply in shock?

Finally, he pointed up to the Big Dipper directly over our campsite and sleepily observed, "You know what, Dad? That real bright star could be first base, and that one over there could be third base, and that spot in the middle could be the pitcher's mound, and. . . ."

I learned that night that it doesn't all happen at once, and that one of the best ways you can raise teenagers is simply to be there for them—when "you sit at home and when you walk along the road, when you lie down and when you get up" (Deuteronomy 6:7).

Some of my most precious family memories are those late night talks in my teenagers' bedrooms when they open up and reveal their inner worlds. Fortunately, that anxiety-producing lecture that I gave to my son developed into a series of great discussions about sex as he matured and saw that I was available to him.

It is possible for you to be a parent and a solid Christian friend to your teen at the same time. God has a good track record for healing broken relationships and strengthening existing ones.

CHAPTER
6

If Ugly Was a Crime, I'd Have Been Born in Jail

Reason #4: Low self-esteem

Mᴏʀᴇ ᴛʜᴀɴ ᴏɴᴄᴇ I ʜᴀᴠᴇ received a teen-written letter that I wished could have found its way into the hands—and hearts—of the parents before it reached mine.

Dear Bob,

I saw you this past weekend at the New York State Youth Convention. I really wanted to talk to you, but I chickened out. I find it easier to write things on paper.

I've been in a depression since school started. These past few weeks have gotten so bad that suicide has become dominant in my thoughts. It is really scaring me because I don't want to die, but I do at the same time. I cry myself to sleep just about every night, praying at the same time that God will let me die.

There are many things that have led to it. My father's

work has become hard for him, so that when he comes home, he's always in a bad mood. He and my mother fight a lot. It gets to the point where she has started to cry, and I've never seen her cry before. The rest of us are really edgy because of that, so we fight too.

I'm doing bad in school, so I'm getting a lot of pressure from my teachers, and I can't handle it right now. My first report card came today, and I haven't shown my parents yet. I'm afraid to.

Another thing that has gotten to me is that I am eighteen years old and I have never had a real boyfriend. I guess it's because I'm so ugly! If I were a guy, I wouldn't want me, either.

Sometimes I feel like giving myself out sexually so I would feel like someone cared about me. I JUST WANT TO BE LOVED.

Today was so bad for me, I just wanted to go to sleep and never wake up again, but that's too easy. If I didn't know the consequences, I'd take a knife to my wrist or a gun to my head right now. Maybe someday I'll get up the nerve to go through with it. Maybe soon. Maybe tomorrow. Everyday I get more nerve.

It's not like I haven't tried before—I just haven't been lucky enough to die.

Thanks for letting me get my thoughts out on paper. Please write me—I NEED A FRIEND.

In *Five Cries of Youth*, Merton Strommen surveyed over 7,000 high school students and discovered that the most commonly voiced and intensely felt of the five cries was the cry of self-hatred. Strommen reported that the main contributing factors to this cry were distress over personal faults, lack of self-confidence, and low self-regard.[1]

I attempted to measure this problem among the teens in

my study to see if there was any correlation between a poor self-image and rejection of religion. I found low self-esteem to be the fourth highest predictor of teen alienation from the church. Average responses from the 400 randomly selected students surveyed were:

"I am an attractive person." (disagree)
"I do poorly in sports and games." (agree)
"I am a morally weak person." (undecided)
"I am satisfied to be just who I am." (strongly disagree)
"I am not happy with myself." (agree)
"I am not loved by my family." (undecided)

THE LONELINESS FACTOR

Craig Ellison claims, "Among all the problems facing teenagers, loneliness is one of the most important." A professor of psychology at Simpson College, he conducted research among fifteen- to nineteen-year-olds. In his estimation, there are two critical causes of loneliness among teenagers:

1. *Teens feel a lack of belonging or fitting in.*
2. *Teens feel that no one cares enough to understand them.*[2]

I agree with Ellison that teens are particularly susceptible to feeling isolated from God, parents, peers, and especially from themselves. A lack of belonging in any of these key relationships or the sense of being misunderstood can produce destructive loneliness.

Do you remember what it was like to feel alone and misunderstood at a time in your life when you weren't sure who you were or what you were worth? Dennis Varden, sixteen years old, knew that feeling. He wrote this piece of prose just before he took his own life.

> *He always wanted to have things explained,*
> *But no one cared.*
> *The teacher came and spoke to him.*
> *She told him to wear a tie like all the other little boys.*
> *He asked, "What does it really matter?"*

After that they drew.
He drew all yellow—
It was the way he felt about the morning
And it was beautiful.
But the teacher came and looked at him.
"What's this?" she said.
"Why don't you draw something like Ken's drawing?
Isn't his picture beautiful?"
After that his mother bought him a tie.
And he always drew airplanes and rocket ships
Like everyone else.
And he threw his old picture away.
But he wasn't alive anymore.
He was square inside and brown.
And his hands were still.
And he was like everyone else.
And the things inside him that needed saying
Didn't need it anymore.
It had stopped pushing.
It was crushed.
Stiff.
Like everything else.

NOBODY AND NO BODY

At the same time that teenagers are feeling that nobody cares or understands, they are also taking a critical look at their bodies and, more often than not, are further depressed by what they see.

Elizabeth Hurlock in her book *Developmental Psychology* notes that very few adolescents experience body-cathexis, or satisfaction with their bodies. She adds, "This failure to be satisfied with who you are physically is one of the causes of unfavorable self-concepts and lack of self-esteem during the adolescent years."[3]

According to Hurlock, there are three basic body types

accompanied by predictable levels of self-esteem. More than likely you will see your teen in one of them:

1. THE MESOMORPH—"well-built"; having more muscular than adipose tissue, this teen usually finds personal and social success more easily than the other two body types.

2. THE ENDOMORPH—obese; having more adipose than muscular tissue, this youth often is ridiculed by his peers and pitied by adults.

3. THE ECTOMORPH—"skinny", with small muscles and little adipose tissue, this teen is often socially maladjusted and exhibits an obsession with his physical appearance.[4]

I can empathize with teens on this subject because I had such a struggle with accepting my own physique. I was the self-conscious ectomorph. With religious zeal I would descend to my basement nightly for a rendezvous with my no-money-back Charles Atlas course: push-ups, sit-ups, jumping jacks, and four-count burpies.

After working up a good sweat with the calisthenics, I got down to serious business with the weight-training. With all the strength I could muster, I powered that weight-lifting bar up, up, up, and jerked it cleanly over my head in triumph. Then I set the bar down, put the weights back on it, and rolled it into the corner. I was going to be the biggest, strongest athlete in my school!

One day during lunch hour, I was unintentionally standing near a group of the popular guys in the hallway, feeling insecure as usual and desperately wanting to fit in. Emerging from the cafeteria came a girl on whom I had a secret crush.

To my surprise, she walked right up to me and said, "Hi, Bob."

In front of the guys, I self-consciously stammered, "Uhh-h-h, H-Hi, Doris."

I had no idea what else to say and was relieved when everybody started in talking again. I felt good about her seeing me with those "cool dudes" and wished that there was something I could do to impress her. Just then the bell rang and, as things started to break up, Doris moved toward me and casually placed her hand on my right arm to say good-bye.

Instinctively my arm went into a rigid flex, and she exclaimed in front of everybody, "Wow! You've really got a muscle there."

I should have left well enough alone, but without thinking I crowed, "Yeah, I've been working out. C'mon, Doris. Hit me in the stomach as hard as you want. It won't even hurt me."

This was too good to miss. Late for class or not, the crowd seemed to swell as it gathered around us. It was then that I remembered something—Doris was one of the best athletes in our school. She was not only pretty; she was strong.

"Are you serious, Bob? I can hit you as hard as I want?"

"No problem," I replied, but the beads on my forehead betrayed the quiver in my liver.

She reared back, wound up, and buried her fist in my middle; then she pulled back, waiting for me to fold.

I looked at her as straight as I could with crossed eyes and repeated through clenched teeth, "*no problem*!"

It seems to be a phenomenon of adolescence that no matter how intelligent a teen is, he often feels very dumb; no matter how attractive, she often feels ugly; no matter how many people are concerned about them, they often feel unloved.

DEFINING THE HEALTHY SELF-IMAGE

Stanley Coopersmith suggests four main components of a teenager's healthy self-image:

1. SIGNIFICANCE—Your teens need to feel important to people who matter to them.

2. COMPETENCE—They must believe that they can do

something well that makes a genuine contribution and is important to them.

3. POWER—They need to feel that they have some control over their lives—that they have some decision-making capacities.

4. VIRTUE—They must believe that they are doing what they know to be right.[5]

Coopersmith has dealt with the social, physical, mental, and moral aspects of self-esteem, but he has neglected the spiritual. As a Christian educator, I would add a fifth component to his construct:

5. PEACE—They must feel that their search for purpose and meaning in life has found its object in a personal experience with God in Jesus Christ.

Parents would scarcely be human if they didn't worry about the hard moral choices that their teens are facing every day in their absence. But ironically, the parents who are most worried about the ethical behavior of their teenagers are often the same ones who have, by engendering low self-esteem in their teens, made it very difficult for them to make good choices.

Stone and Church remind us that "it is not usually the person who has developed self-respect who turns into a doormat or a punching-bag for others."[6] It is unlikely that a teen with poor self-image will consistently have the strength of will to say no to drugs, premarital sex, drinking, and other negative options readily available to today's teenagers.

In his book, *Human Development in Western Culture,* Bernard states, "When children feel they are worthy of consideration, when limits are firm but established without parental condemnation, when encouragement rather than censure follows errors, the individual achieves a [strong] self-image. . . . It is this self-image that develops the internalization of moral codes and becomes one's conscience. . . . *Basic to the establishment of a set of ethical values is a strong self-concept.*"[7]

WHAT PARENTS CAN DO

Even though your teen has to drive the old family station wagon and still shares a room with his little brother, if self-respect keeps his head held high, then you are a parent who should be content.

Even though you can't afford to buy her the latest styles with the right labels, and she may never be elected to the homecoming court, if she likes who she is and is excited about who she is becoming, then you are a parent who should be grateful.

If you do nothing else for your teens but to equip them with confidence to, as James Cavanaugh writes, "live among the wolves," then you are a parent who should be revered.

"If you desire to be a helper of young people—a counselor in the best sense of the word, regardless of your technical training—here is one of your most vital tasks. You must help teenagers to accept themselves, to like themselves, to be glad they are who they are, to realize their value."[8]

How do you begin? Here are several things you can do to help build self-esteem in your teenagers:

1. Give them a sense of belonging.

"Once you were less than nothing; now you are God's own. Once you knew very little of God's kindness; now your very lives have been changed by it" (I Peter 2:10, LB).

Fitting into most of the social groups which make up the teenager's world almost always depends upon performance, looks, economic standing, or conformity. If your son is athletic enough, he is sure to find acceptance among the school "jocks." If your daughter is attractive, other-centered, and willing to conform to the American dating system, she can count on popularity among her peers.

There is only one group which does not—or at least should not—insist that teens measure up to its expectations before they are accepted: that is the family. It is possible for you to make your home that one place where your teenagers can fit in—in spite of an acne problem, empty wallet, fumbled football, bouts with depression, or an inability to grasp advanced algebra.

2. *Resist the urge to recount your former successes.*

"Speak only what is helpful for building others up according to their needs" (Ephesians 4:29b).

Zig Ziglar reminds us that when we rehearse our accomplishments from the past with our teens, "time dramatically improves [our] performance."[9] It is not uncommon for teens to become so discouraged with trying to live up to the quixotic stories and embellished achievements of their parents' past that they opt for destructive behavior.

Competing with the past, even if it is not an illusion, is too unrealistic a burden to lay on any teenager. So avoid the temptation to finish any sentence which begins with, "What do you mean you can't do it? Why, when I was your age—" or "I'm not one to brag, but—."

Your teens are bound to learn about your past laurels from old high-school yearbooks, casual banter at family reunions, and diaries that turn up when you pack to move to a new house. If they discover your credits on their own, it is liable to endear you to them and give them a sense of healthy pride. But if you preach your past to them, do not be surprised by their resentment and alienation. Better that you discretely share your blunders than your boasts with your teenagers.

3. *Caution them frequently that no one can steal their self-worth without their permission.*

"It is God himself who has made us what we are and given us new lives from Christ Jesus" (Ephesians 2:10a, LB).

Neither you nor your teen is responsible for how others mistreat you, but you are accountable for how you react to slander, unjust criticism, and a vindictive spirit.

I had a student with a history of low self-esteem. He was aware of his susceptibility to depression triggered by anyone who criticized his efforts. We talked often about how his true self-worth was derived not from his performance, nor from the opinions of others, but from the fact that God had made him who he was. He had to stop allowing people or circumstances to steal his self-esteem.

One day in my office, I saw the lights go on in his head and a smile come across his face. It was not long afterwards that I heard he had placed a poster with three meaningful words over the bookshelf in his dorm room: *Don't allow it!*

Saint Augustine once observed, "People travel to wonder at the height of mountains, at the huge waves of the sea, at the long courses of the rivers, at the vast compass of the ocean, at the circular motion of the stars—and they pass by themselves without wondering."[10]

4. *It's never too late to focus on your teenager's inner qualities.*

"Be beautiful inside, in your hearts, with the lasting beauty of a gentle and quiet spirit which is so precious to God" (I Peter 3:4, LB).

We learned not to expect much in the way of physical attractiveness in our newborns for the first few weeks. Though they grow into fine looking children, each of our babies has been characterized by a head remarkably misshapen from its trip down the birth canal, a scalp as hairless as a billiard ball, and a funny little scowl that could curdle Similac. Cabbage Patch "preemies" have nothing on any of them.

So when our third child was born, I stood outside the hospital nursery window watching the nurse bathe her, thanking God for the smooth delivery, rejoicing in her good health, and praying for God to help us raise our daughter to be a committed Christian woman. Presently a fellow member of the church softball team came along to view the baby and congratulate me.

It was humorous for me to see him taking in that lopsided head, bald pate, wrinkled brow, and toothless scowl. Not knowing me very well, I'm sure he felt that he had to say something appropriate. He went beyond the call of duty.

"Hey, hey! What a beauty, huh? You're going to have a hard time keeping the guys away from that one. She's going to be a real heartbreaker!"

I knew that he meant no harm, but his comment got me thinking about the imbecilic system we have for evaluating human worth in this country. Almost from the day of their births, we condition our sons and daughters to believe that their self-worth is wrapped up in their physical appearance.

I overheard a young woman say that girls do not spend all that time and money on cosmetics because they are dumb or vain. On the contrary, they are intelligent enough to know that guys can see better than they can *think!*

One of the greatest lessons a child can learn is the meaning behind the verse, "The Lord does not see as man sees. Man looks at the outward appearance, but the Lord looks at the heart" (1 Samuel 16:7). It would be a good idea, when we are with our teens, if we could focus on things which last. Perhaps if we took every opportunity to compliment them on their character, integrity, and the fruit of the Spirit as it is evidenced in their lives (see Galatians 5:22, 23), we might see them better handle their struggle with self-esteem.

5. *Help them experience satisfaction and find balance with their physical appearance.*

"Honor God with your body" (I Corinthians 6:20).

As crucial as it is to encourage your teen to focus on his internal qualities, the fact is that there will probably be times when he can't see the "eternal" because the "temporary" is driving him to distraction (see II Corinthians 4:18: "So we fix our eyes not on what is seen, but on what is unseen. For what is seen is temporary, but what is unseen is eternal").

Having a teenager who is inordinately vain about his good looks is a problem. But is it less vain or destructive for a teen to be self-consumed with what he considers to be a physical flaw? I was extremely self-conscious and rendered socially dysfunctional in my early teen years by a chipped front tooth. After being teased by some kids at school about my "Bucky Beaver" grin, it became difficult for me to look people straight on when talking with them, and I eventually developed a crooked smile which remains with me today. My confidence level skyrocketed the weekend I had my teeth capped.

Whether you need to connect with an orthodontist for braces, an optometrist for contact lenses, a dermatologist for skin care, or even a plastic surgeon for help with a crooked nose, your teen's appreciation will make the expense worth it. It may free them up to go deeper when they are no longer plagued by a surface problem.

6. Remind them often of their inestimable worth.

"This is love: not that we loved God, but that he loved us and sent his Son as an atoning sacrifice for our sins" (I John 4:10).

I believe that it is God's desire that our teens value themselves in accordance with the price He has placed upon them. Your teenager is worth the death of Jesus Christ.

My sixteen-year-old son and I have a better understanding of that price because of a severely broken leg he suffered in a skiing accident when he was seven. For some reason there was no doctor available to set his bone on that raw February evening, so the decision was made to get him through the night with pain shots.

My nerves were on edge and my heart breaking with compassion as I sat in his darkened hospital room, listening to his quiet weeping turn to crying and eventually to feverish screaming. I felt totally helpless and gladly would have offered both of my legs for breaking if it would have alleviated the smallest part of his suffering.

Eventually, the pain was so intense and his fear of another hypodermic needle so vivid that he called me over to his bed. "Dad," he begged me, "you've got to promise me something!"

"What is it, son?" I replied, unable any longer to restrain my own tears.

"Don't let them stick me again!" he implored.

Scarcely a moment later, the nurse called me into the hallway and said, "Mr. Laurent, your son is waking this whole wing up. I have instructions to help him get to sleep."

I was relieved to hear that and wondered why they hadn't done so earlier. "Fine," I answered. "How are you going to do it?"

"I have to give him another injection. I need you to hold him down for me."

I pinned my son's spindly arms to the bed as the nurses whipped the sheet off his body and, for the fifth time that night, jabbed him in his bottom with the hypodermic.

His eyes were as big as saucers as he stared at me and let out a scream that pierced me like cold steel: "DA-A-A-A-A-ADD!"

For the first time in my life, I understood the Father's side of the Cross.

The day before His death at Golgotha, Jesus informed His best friends that he would be crucified and that, in the end, even they would betray them. They were vehement in their denial and pledged their loyalty to Him. In view of what happened on Friday, His next words surely came from the human side of the God-Man. "But I will not be alone, for my Father will be with me."

Jesus spoke several times as He hung on the Cross for six hours between Heaven and Hell. But to me, His most poignant speech occurred at the moment He fully realized the price which sin was to exact. Bleeding to death for the sins of the world, He became aware of something which had never happened since before the dawn of time. *"My God! My God! Why have you forsaken me?"*

Did God the Father hear his only Son crying, "DA-A-A-ADD!" when, because Jesus became my sin, His own father turned away from Him?

If I, having been created in the image of God, instinctively was ready to sacrifice all of my limbs that night just to repair my son's leg, what might the Father-heart of God felt on the dark afternoon His Son was murdered? The more basic question, though, is, why did He allow it?

The answer for you and your teenager is that you both are worth the death of Jesus Christ. You are that much loved.

CHAPTER

7

Youth Pastor or Superman?

Reason #5: Poor relationship with youth pastor

"IF YOU WANT TO INFLUENCE A teenager, you've got to establish a relationship with him," says Dan Spader of Moody's Sonlife Ministries. He describes an effective youth ministry as "primarily relational. Secular educators have demonstrated that children twelve years and younger are primarily influenced by rewards and punishments, while mature adults are motivated through cognitive thinking and stimulating ideas. But *teens determine what's true based on what they experience in relationships*" [emphasis mine].[1]

My research revealed that the bond between church-going teens and their youth pastor (or any other adult working with the high school youth ministry) is highly correlated with their acceptance or rejection of Christianity. In fact, the teens surveyed cited their feelings about their youth pastors as the fifth leading cause for them either to stay active in or turn away from the church. Their average responses were:

"My youth pastor is more interested in his paycheck than he is in me." (disagree)

"I get along well with my youth pastor." (undecided)

"I feel free to talk frankly about personal concerns with my youth pastor." (disagree)

"My youth pastor is really interested in me personally." (undecided)

"My youth pastor acts as though a teenager knows practically nothing." (disagree)

"My youth pastor does not seem to understand me." (agree)

"Once my youth pastor makes a decision, nothing could make him change his mind. (agree)

"My youth pastor will apologize to a teen if he has made a mistake." (disagree)

"My youth pastor is usually too busy to help me." (agree)

In a study attempting to understand why some teenagers develop stronger faith patterns than others, Michael Mason found that active members of church youth programs displayed a number of common characteristics: supportive parents, some type of emotional "faith experience," and a significant relationship with another adult for whom faith was important and meaningful.[2]

For my own two teenagers, that "significant adult" has been their youth pastor. Their weekly (and in the summer almost daily) contact with him has increased their enthusiasm for the church and visibly strengthened their faith.

This study demonstrates that next to a teen's parents, a youth pastor (or intimate adult youth sponsor) has the most influence on a teenager's faith—apparently even greater than peer influence. Taking advantage of the free-response item in the questionnaire, several teens affirmed the crucial role that a youth pastor has played in their lives.

I love the church I'm going to. Our youth pastor is really cool.

Mine is not just a church where you go every once in a while, but where you really want to go. We have a great youth pastor.

I love our youth pastor and want to do the same thing with my life when I'm older.

The high school students I interviewed named several characteristics they are looking for in a youth pastor:

1. Availability
2. Acceptance
3. Authenticity, both in character and in faith
4. Vulnerability
5. Sensitivity

In the arena of youth ministry today, there is a healthy movement away from "model" roles to genuine vulnerability and humanness. Most youth accept more quickly adults who readily concede that they are still "in process," that they do not have all the answers, and that they are susceptible to failure.

In the same regard, the youth pastor should not feel the need to protect the teens from grappling with hard questions about their faith. On the contrary, teens should have the opportunity to experience Christianity as a rational, thinking faith which can stand up to the kind of honest questioning that typifies the adolescent mind.

Teens need a pastor friend with whom they can be true to their own stage of cognitive development. Adolescence is a time for the kind of questioning and doubting that can be crucial to faith development. They must develop their own personal convictions about Christianity.

WHAT'S A PARENT TO DO?

Working closely with churches across the country, I have learned much about the enigmatic life of a youth pastor. Consider the bewildering position that many youth pastors find themselves in:

If his hair has any gray in it, he is too old to relate to teenagers. If he is a recent graduate, he hasn't had enough experience for the job.

If he has any children, he has too many distractions. If he has no children, he can't relate to the parents of his teens.

If his wife takes an active role in his ministry, she is a presuming woman and doesn't know her place. If she doesn't, she is not interested in the church.

If he makes a few close friends, he is cliquish. If he is friendly with everyone, he is insincere and shallow.

If he gets along well with the youth and has fun doing his job, he's not mature enough. If he displays his frustration with their apathy and presses them toward discipleship, he takes himself too seriously and is hard to get along with.

If he considers someday pastoring his own church, he's not committed to helping youth. If he commits himself to youth work for life, it's because he doesn't have what it takes to be a senior pastor.

Is it any wonder that the mortality rate among youth pastors is so high? Or that American youth put the profession of clergy near the bottom of a list of occupations they would like to enter, ranking it just a cut above undertaking?

There is much that you, as the parent of a teenager, can do to encourage your youth pastor.

1. *Treat him as if he were a gift from God.*

The youth pastor is not your personal spiritual lackey, destined to do your bidding. Neither is he the "hired man" recruited by the church to fill a nebulous office called "youth pastor." According to Scripture and contrary to traditional opinion, the youth pastor does not "take a job" with the church, merely succeeding the last holder of that office. Ephesians 4 records that from His ascended position, the Lord Jesus Christ gave your youth pastor to the church as a gift.

In the past, if a church was disenchanted with a pastor who was not exactly what they wanted, they either voted him out at the first opportunity or decided to ride out his "lame-duck ministry" with as little support or involvement as possible, being satisfied to accomplish almost nothing for the Kingdom. The outcome was often characterized by many hurt feelings and a poorly impressed community of non-Christians. How might the flow of God's Spirit in our churches be increased if we began to view our pastors as genuine gifts from God, and treated them accordingly?

2. Protect his spirit.

How would you like to have a hundred people or so analyzing your every move and judging your performance by what is often little more than their own subjective feelings about you? Neither would I. And yet this kind of pressure is the common experience of youth pastors.

A youth pastor has far more opportunity to have his spirit crushed and confidence shattered than many of us. The hundreds of young men and women who flee the ministry for secular jobs is a tragic commentary on the lack of love that we reserve for the clergy. It is time to grasp the meaning behind Proverbs 18:14, "A man's spirit will bear him up during his infirmity; but a wounded spirit, who can bear?"

3. Give him room to be human.

It has always seemed unreasonable to me that we Christians are so long-suffering with nonbelievers, but almost merciless when one of the clergy occasionally fails us.

We do not need to be known as the only army that shoots its own wounded.

It will help to recognize from the start of his ministry that, because he struggles with the same sin nature that you do, your youth pastor stands in constant need of God's grace and yours. We must not set him up so high that the image is smashed when we see his humanity showing through—nor so low that he is merely our "buddy" with whom we exchange meaningless jokes.

We must forgive him when he sins against us and pray for his growth. But if he offends us because his preaching and lifestyle confront us with our sins, he does not need our forgiveness nor our criticism.

4. Pay him well.

I've noticed through the years that when a church is looking for a youth pastor, they usually want someone with the strength of an eagle, the grace of a swan, the gentleness of a dove, the friendliness of a sparrow, the eye of a hawk, the night hours of an owl—and who can live on the food of a canary!

Please, don't let your church do your youth pastor's sacrificing for him. Allow him the joy of giving also. Your congregation might see a whole lot more grain tread out if it would quit muzzling the ox (see I Tim. 5:18). More than one church has unwittingly extinguished the fire in their youth program by being stingy with the youth pastor's salary.

5. Give him freedom to follow the Spirit.

Not all of the traditions which we hold sacred are actually biblical norms for the New Testament Church. In many churches, the order of service in the bulletin has become "holy writ," and God help the poor preacher who tampers with it.

If your church is gifted with a youth pastor whose vision is fresh and whose spirit is ready to do new things for the Kingdom, don't quench him with, "But it's never been done that way before!" Consider yourselves blessed by God if your youth pastor wants to pioneer new trails, and get behind him when he does.

6. *Defend his right to privacy, and if he is married, to a strong home life.*

The divorce rate among young ministers is alarming but not surprising. It seems that if a youth pastor is not strong-willed to the point of offending many, he ends up spending a great deal more time attending to his teenage congregation's needs than to those of his own family. This is one of the main reasons it is so difficult to be married to a youth pastor and probably why so many preacher's kids are known for their rebellious behavior. It doesn't take long for his mate or children to figure out who is number one in the pastor's life. If the Lord takes that position, then the family will run a close second, and the youth ministry a more effective third.

7. *Encourage your teens to get involved in the work of the church.*

I have seen a number of youth pastors become discouraged to the point of quitting because they can count only on themselves and a few beleaguered adult sponsors to do most of the work of the youth ministry. The major portion of his work load should be to equip the teenagers of your church for the work of the ministry (Ephesians 4:12).

He is the shepherd/enabler; your teens are the sheep/workers. It is from the wool of their involvement that the fibre of the church's youth ministry must be spun.

8. *Look for opportunities to support him.*

Normally there are a few people in each church who vie

with the youth pastor for control of the direction of the youth program. Their line of thinking is often, "We were here when he came, and we'll still be here long after he's gone."

Although everyone has the right to be heard and valued, no one has the right to usurp the youth pastor's leadership role if he is living according to I Timothy 3. We must remember to respect our pastors "and hold them in the highest regard in love because of their work" (I Tim. 5:12, 13).

9. Be his friend.

"It's lonely at the top," said a youth pastor friend recently. "I can honestly say that I do not have one good friend among all of these people that I work with and love."

Just as David needed Jonathan, and Paul needed Silas, your youth pastor needs you. If it is possible, befriend him and his wife. They need to be loved . . . just like you.

A youth pastor cannot function effectively without encouragement and understanding from the parents of the teens that he loves. Have you hugged your youth pastor today?

CHAPTER
8

A World of "Differents"

Reason #6: Negative peer influence

"In the 1940's the teacher's main problems with students were talking, running in the halls, and chewing gum in class. Today the problems are different—assault, vandalism, teen pregnancy, and drug and alcohol abuse." So says Josh McDowell in *Network News.*[1] My own experiences confirm that he is not overstating his case.

"Hey, Bob! Please come here. We need to ask you something."

I had just lectured to a teenage audience on "The Difference between Love and Sex," and their assignment now was to divide into small groups and discuss some questions I'd given them. I turned to see half a dozen junior high girls sitting in a circle on the gymnasium floor. I walked over to them and said, "What can I do for you ladies?"

The girl who had gotten my attention asked, "Did you mean what you said today about a guy wanting to marry a virgin?"

"Yes, I think that when most young men get serious about marriage, they would like to find a girl they could trust, a girl who has not been 'passed around' by their buddies, a girl whose name and phone number was not scrawled on a stall in the boys' bathroom."

There was silence. In a matter of seconds, several of the girls in that group were quietly crying. I didn't know what to say, so, following their lead, I stared at the gym floor and said nothing for a while. I was having a hard time believing that seventh and eighth graders could be sexually "experienced."

"You girls are only in junior high. Do you mean that there's already that much pressure on you to have sex?"

Against the backdrop of her friends' sniffling, one girl gave an angry reply, punctuated by her own tears. "It's not fair," she said. "You have no idea how the guys at our school make you feel if you don't put out. The pressure is incredible."

A recent survey of 900 teenagers by *Seventeen* magazine revealed that:

Over seventy-five percent used birth control.

Thirty-seven percent of the girls and fifty-eight percent of the boys said there is nothing wrong with premarital intercourse and "I intend to try it or have done it."

Only twenty-two percent of the girls and sixteen percent of the boys said that sex before marriage was a bad idea.[2]

Unfortunately, Christian teenagers appear to be no exception. Research shows that by twelfth grade, sixty-two percent of today's churched teens have been sexually involved.[3]

As difficult as it is to believe now, there was a day when dating a girl meant getting dressed up, bringing her a gift like candy or flowers, seeing her under the parental roof, and leaving her home at a designated time. Just as carefully proscribed was sexual conduct during the date. Kissing and heavy petting were considered boorish if not outright forbidden until the couple was actually engaged.

Liberal social attitudes toward sex, the legalization of abortion, and the availability of contraceptives have radically changed the sexual behavior of teenagers today. Hurlock states, "There are many reasons for this new pattern of sexual behavior. Among these are the belief that it is the 'thing to do' because everyone else does it; that girls and boys who are still virgins by the time they reach their senior year in high school are 'different,' and to adolescents this means 'inferior'; that they must comply with pressures from their peer group if they wish to maintain their status in the group; and that such behavior is an expression of a meaningful relationship which fills the need every adolescent has for a close association with others, especially when this need is not filled by family relationships."[4]

Although premarital sex has a higher visibility than other teenage social problems, smoking, drinking, and the use of drugs are also becoming more characteristic of today's youth culture. These harmful activities usually begin as peer group experiences.

All three are not uncommon at the junior high level and have developed into something of a status symbol for girls as well as boys. Because teenagers spend so much time outside the home with their friends, it is understandable that peers often have a greater influence on adolescent attitudes, speech, appearance and behavior than the family has. If members of the peer group experiment with tobacco, alcohol, and drugs, teenagers are "likely to do the same, regardless of how they feel about these matters."[5]

DEFUSING THE SEX BOMB

Few phenomena concern parents more than the specter of peer pressure driving their children to destructive sexual behavior. Teens, especially during the early phases of adolescence, tend to be a conformist group. Is there anything parents can do to prevent their teenagers from trading the values in which they were raised for the acceptance and approval of their peers?

While there are no guarantees that your teens will stay unsoiled sexually, there are measures which you can take to help them make the right choices.

1. *Treat sex as a positive gift from God.*

"Let him kiss me with the kisses of his mouth—for your love is more delightful than wine" (Song of Solomon 1:2).

I was raised in a home where the subject of sex was never broached. It was a dirty word, and although I was often curious about it, I knew better than to ask questions. But one Saturday night, after observing from my bedroom window my older brother and his girlfriend in a car, I was determined to find out what was going on. I stayed awake until he finally came in from his date.

"What were you guys doing out there?" I asked. "Were you wrestling, or what?"

"Oh, Bobby," came his brusque reply. "It's sex, and you're too young to understand."

Where could I go to find an answer? My parents? No, I was convinced that they never did anything like that. My friends? No, it would be too embarrassing to display my ignorance.

There was only one person with whom I felt secure enough to ask such a question—my favorite Sunday School teacher, Mrs. Murphy. I knew that she liked me, so I waited around until after class the next day and finally worked up the nerve to ask her.

"Mrs. Murphy, could you tell me something, ma'am?"

"Of course, son. What is it?"

"Mrs. Murphy, what is sex?"

It was as if a personality change came over this normally

kindest of teachers. I had invoked the "S-word" in church—not a casual misdemeanor in those days. Her shock gave way to a scowl as she replied, "Bobby Laurent, do you know where little boys go who have sex?"

"Sure," I replied. "Out in the car with my brother Bill."

My quasi-Victorian upbringing served to give me a perverted view of sex and made it almost impossible for me to experience healthy Biblical sex with my own wife. But one of the best things that ever happened to my marriage was hearing Josh McDowell speak. My wife and I were still newlyweds when I first heard him talk on a subject which I had been conditioned to believe Christians were not supposed to discuss.

Sitting in an auditorium with over a thousand other ministers, I jotted down the date, location, and name of the speaker, and waited for him to announce his topic. In his own inimitable style, Josh began, "The title of my message tonight is something that my wife Dotty and I very much believe in: *maximum sex!*" he shouted.

I remember thinking, *I can't write that down. This is a spiritual notebook!*

McDowell proceeded to show us from Scripture that within the protective confines of marriage, sex can be one of the most wonderful experiences God has ever given to man.

"In fact," he announced proudly, "Dotty and I have sex on every day of the week that starts with a 'T'."

While I was trying to figure out which days those were, he bellowed, "Tuesdays, Thursdays, TODAY, TOMOR-ROW . . . TATURDAY and TUNDAY!!"

The clergy-filled hall rocked with laughter.

It was a message I needed to hear, as a Christian and a husband. To the orthodox Jewish husband, making love to his wife was no less spiritual than reciting the Torah. "May your fountain be blessed, and may you rejoice in the wife of your youth. . . . May her breasts satisfy you always, may you ever be captivated by her love" (Proverbs 5:18, 19).

God made us sexual creatures. To incarcerate a teenager from the subject of sex is not the course of wisdom. With the kind of sexual pressure teens face today, such a strategy would only ensure his "coming out party" later on. To teach him that because sex is such a sublime gift from God, its misuse can be devastating, is the saner approach.

2. Don't assume the worst.

"If you love someone you will be loyal to him no matter what the cost. You will always believe in him, always expect the best of him, and always stand your ground in defending him" (I Corinthians 13:7, LB).

"The reason I'm a Christian today," a friend once told me, "is because my parents trusted me when I couldn't be trusted." It wasn't that they allowed him to do anything he wanted. Instead, they communicated their belief in him so effectively that even when he knew he was not worthy of that trust, he could not bring himself to break such a strong bond of love.

If you are constantly suspicious of your teen and accuse him of sexual misconduct when such is not the case, you unwittingly might be guaranteeing illicit sexual behavior in his future.

"My parents think I'm no good anyway," I've heard teens say. "I might as well live 'down' to their expectations."

3. Practice mutual accountability with your teen.

"I made a covenant with my eyes not to look lustfully at a girl" (Job 31:1).

Walking into the living room one day, I saw my teenage son reading on the sofa. When he noticed me, he instinctively closed his book.

Because I did the same thing when my own father walked into my bedroom unannounced many years before, I had an idea of what I would see when I opened the book to the pages which had closed on my son's finger. I must say that I haven't looked at that section of the Penney's catalog for many years and was surprised at the quantity and quality of pictures displaying beautiful women modeling lingerie.

What is the best way for a father to handle such a situation—with a cry of *"Pervert!"* followed by a sound thrashing or grounding for a week?

I sensed a "teachable moment," sat down next to my son, engaged the look of apprehension in his eyes, and said, "So you think you're old enough to wear this stuff now, huh?"

His nervous laugh was better than my comment deserved.

I held up the catalog and remarked, "These pictures are really something, aren't they?"

"Yeah, they sure are, Dad," he replied with cautious relief.

I knew that it was a serious moment, but I couldn't help chuckling. "You want to talk about it?" I asked.

There followed one of those priceless hours when pressures are released, Scriptures are searched, and fathers get closer to sons. We talked about ways to help each other stay sexually pure in a day when the squeeze is on fathers as well as sons to stray from the narrow path. We ended our conversation with prayer and a decision to be mutually accountable to each other for what we allowed our eyes to see.

By the way, you'd be surprised how much easier it is to lift the Penney's catalog without those pages.

4. Prepare them for the power of seductive words.

"For the lips of an adulteress drip honey, and her speech is smoother than oil" (Proverbs 5:3).

According to a survey done by the University of Iowa on teenage sexual behavior, an adolescent girl often experiences premarital intercourse because of her "emotional insecurity drive." As Stinnett and Taylor have explained, "Many youths turn to [sex] in an attempt to find the close relationship which they have not found in their own families."[6]

This could be one of the reasons that teenage boys say "I love you" too quickly and girls believe it too quickly. When they don't receive love at home, there is a higher probability that they will be duped by the illusion of love outside the home.

5. *Remind them of God's forgiveness.*

"For the grace of God . . . teaches us to say no to ungodliness and worldly passions" (Titus 2:11, 12).

No matter what you do to prevent it, there may come a time when you are in a position to reenact with your teenager the scene in which Jesus spoke to the woman caught in adultery. "Does no man condemn you? . . . Neither do I. Go and sin no more" (John 8:10, 11).

I was visited one afternoon by a college student who felt worthless and defeated by a sexual sin for which she had long ago repented. Still the shame of it followed her and rendered her hopeless of ever finding a Christian husband. After listening to her pour out her heart, I played a song for her by Leslie Phillips. The chorus goes, "It's Your kindness that leads us to repentance, O Lord. Knowing that You love us, no matter what we do makes us want to love You too."

Understanding God's forgiveness was the beginning of her long trip back to self-respect and hope for the future.

WHEN THE PEER GROUP IS THE REAL WORLD

Negative peer influence is a major reason that teenagers reject religion. Following are the mean responses of the teens in the study to the items which measured the influence of negative peer pressure on adolescent alienation from the church.

"I am more likely to act like a Christian when I'm with my Christian friends and to act like a non-Christian when I'm with my non-Christian friends." (agree)

"I get upset when my non-Christian friends leave me out of their activities." (agree)

"I'd rather be with my friends than with my family." (agree)

"I try to keep up with the latest fads." (strongly agree)

"My non-Christian friends' opinions are important to me." (strongly agree)

"If I needed advice, I'd ask my friends before I asked my parents." (agree)

"It bothers me when my non-Christian friends think I'm too religious." (agree)

"My non-Christian friends have a strong influence on me." (undecided)

For many adolescents, the peer group is the real world—a world in which they may socialize in a climate where the values are determined not by adults, but by their equals. If their friends care little or nothing for religion, it is unrealistic to expect teenagers to be enthusiastic about their faith or active in their church.

MAKING PEER PRESSURE POSITIVE

In spite of the potentially negative influence of peer pressure, Bruce Narramore reminds us that the process behind it is completely natural and God-given. "Our teenagers are susceptible to their friends' influence, because they are in the process of weaning themselves from us and learning to think for themselves. For years they have grounded their identities in parental relationships. What we said and did was pretty much what they accepted as right or true or proper. But physical and intellectual growth incite independent action and thought. Part of the process of maturing is learning to think for oneself and being open to the influence of one's friends."[7]

If peer influence is a social phenomenon which we are going to have with us, perhaps it is more sensible to make our peace with it. Then, instead of fighting it to a standoff, maybe we can learn ways to make peer pressure work for us.

1. Pray for your teens to make solid Christian friends.

The wisest of men said, "He who walks with the wise grows wise, but a companion of fools suffers harm" (Proverbs 13:20). No parents wish their teenagers to come to harm, but how many of us pray diligently for God to lead our teens into wholesome friendships with Christ-centered peers?

When our family moved to the Chicago area, my wife and I daily asked God to supply each of our children with at least one close Christian friend, so that they would not be alone when trying to influence their non-Christian friends. God answered that prayer.

When Larry Richards mentions the need which every Christian teen has for supportive relationships within his peer group, he is not referring to a large group of friends. On the contrary, "just one or two other teens who share his values is enough to give the teen encouragement and strength in handling the pressures."[8]

2. Make friends with your teens' friends.

For over a decade, one of my worst mistakes as a father was to treat my children's friends with an icy reserve. I wasn't even aware that I was doing it, until one day I asked Joyce why our kids always had to go to their friends' houses to play.

I was shocked when she replied, "Probably because you

don't make them feel very comfortable when they're here."

Although it hurt, I knew that she was right. As much as I loved our children, I was actually forcing them out of our home by not genuinely welcoming their friends.

The reasons for my aloofness were many. Maybe I felt that their friends were slowly taking them away from me. Or maybe I suffered from the "No kid is good enough for my kid" mentality. Or maybe I was just plain selfish and didn't want to bother with any extra bodies around. Whatever the reasons were, they were as pathetic as they were wrong.

I have since learned to feel comfortable around my teens' friends and really enjoy having them in our home. They sense my goodwill, and I believe that somehow it adds a healthy dimension to their friendships with my children.

3. *Build up the confidence of your teenagers.*

Barry St. Clair claims that there are two major reasons why teens submit to negative peer pressure. First, a poor self-image makes adolescents extremely susceptible. They have a strong desire for others to agree with them. Some teens actually develop what might be called a sixth sense which enables them to discern others' expectations so that they can act accordingly. Teenagers with this tendency often forego establishing their own unique identities to conform to behavior that is acceptable to their peers.

Secondly, fear in a teen may express itself in many ways: a fear of offending any peer with an opposing viewpoint or lifestyle; a fear that Christianity will be too rigid and confining, limiting the teen's capacity for fun; or a fear of losing friendships if the teen is seen as being too "religious."[9] The teenager who is sure of himself and what he believes has a much better chance of withstanding negative peer pressure.

4. *Don't allow church to become an "adult institution."*

In his study of adolescence, Ernest Smith observed that

the conflict between adolescent and adult institutions is relieved by the withdrawal of youth from adult institutions (for example, the church). A complex youth culture (often in opposition to the adult institution) then evolves to fill in the socialization gap caused by their withdrawal.[10] One method of defusing this problem would be to eliminate teenagers' need to withdraw by making quite certain that the church never becomes an "adult institution."

It is a central thesis of this book that the church must include teenagers in its power structure and mission—not just to keep them from leaving the church, or even because we desperately need them, but because it is, in every way, the right thing to do.

CHAPTER
9

This Hurts Me More Than It Hurts You

Reason #7: Authoritarianism in parents

A faith which today has to lean on authoritarianism will collapse tomorrow under the pressure of cultural change."—PIERRE BABIN

AUTHORITARIANISM IN churches as well as in parents is a factor in leading teenagers to turn away from their faith. When asked to finish the sentence, "The feelings I have when I think about my religion are—," several of the teenagers in the study revealed alienation from the restrictive aspects of Christianity.

I don't like the standards and attitudes of my church. I will probably switch religions after I graduate.

Most of what I want to do the church says is wrong. I want to be able to live my life and not be criticized every time I do something the church doesn't like.

The church is overcomplicated with rules and not as Christlike as it should be.

I'm not able to be myself; I'm always wondering what others will think.

We spend so much time thinking of what we can or can't do that we don't have time to enjoy life.

Studies of juvenile delinquents reveal that punishment (not to be confused with discipline) not only fails to deter misbehavior but often provokes it.

When I was younger, my brother Mike and I shared a bedroom. It was one of those classy "all-boy" rooms with bunk beds, pennants, posters on the walls, old Wheaties cultures growing underneath the desk, and an ENTER AT YOUR OWN RISK sign on the door. Almost every night at bedtime, our parents would warn us, "Now you kids get right to sleep. No talking—or else!"

We usually obeyed, because we knew these orders had the fastest belt in the Midwest behind them. But one evening, which a certain area of my body can still remember, we reaped what we sowed: TROUBLE.

It started out innocently enough. We were whispering, and Mom heard us from the living room.

"Bobby! Mikey! I thought I told you kids to be quiet! Now pipe down!"

"Yes, ma'am," said the top bunk.

"Yes, ma'am," said the bottom bunk.

We could tell she meant business because of the way her voice cracked when it got high. We knew better than to push it any further. But have you ever had a quiet pillow fight?

We tried to keep the noise down, but Mike kept hitting his head on the ceiling. It was only a matter of time. . . .

"Robert!! Michael!! I thought we told you to go to sleep! One more peep, and it's the belt!"

I could feel Dad's vibrations coming right through the wall.

"Yes, ma'am," from the top bunk.

"Yes, ma'am," from the bottom bunk.

"Don't you 'Yes, ma'am,' me!" from the living room.

"Yes, ma'am."

Now that was dumb! Dad didn't even bother to say,

"This is going to hurt me more than it's going to hurt you, son." He knew better!

Although I believe it is legitimate to spank a child in the right circumstances (see Proverbs 13:24 and 23:13), there comes a time when corporal discipline is inappropriate. The teenage years demand that a parent grow in his understanding of discipline.

Ernest Ligon warns, "Building a successful home is not just a matter of effort. Some of the most heartbreaking tragedies I have seen have taken place in homes in which the parents almost literally ate their hearts out for their children, and still failed tragically. . . . It is because they didn't know how to discipline."[1]

YOU NEVER OUTGROW YOUR NEED FOR DISCIPLINE

Your children experience their own special "passages" which are very important to them.

At age five, they are deemed old enough to ride to kindergarten on a bus without you sitting next to them.

At age ten, they can stay up a half hour later than their six-year-old sister.

At thirteen, nylons, mascara, deodorant and Polo cologne mark a new social awareness.

Their sixteenth year looms before them as THE YEAR of the driver's license. They not only don't need you sitting next to them, they don't even need the bus anymore.

At what age do they no longer need discipline? Is there a magic age when boundaries are to be pushed out so far that your teenagers are on their own?

On the evening of a day she had been spanked, one of my daughters crawled up on my lap and gave me a hug. I appreciated that, because I have never enjoyed having to discipline a child. Then she cupped my face in her hands and with a frown, said, "It's not fair, Daddy. It's really not fair."

"What's not fair, sugar?" I asked.

"Who spanks you?"

With no hesitation, I replied, "God spanks me, honey," and then I explained. The Bible is filled with Scriptures which indicate the importance of discipline.

"Every branch that does bear fruit he prunes so that it will be even more fruitful" (John 15:2).

"The evil deeds of a wicked man ensnare him; He will die for lack of discipline" (Proverbs 5:22, 23).

"My son, do not make light of the Lord's discipline . . . because the Lord disciplines those he loves" (Hebrews 12:5, 6).

Sometimes the Lord uses a concerned friend to discipline me, sometimes a pastor or one of my students ("As iron sharpens iron, so one man sharpens another" Proverbs 27:17). But often God gets my attention through my wife.

Early in our marriage, I decided I would ask her to help me detect any blind spots in my character. I took her to a nice restaurant and made sure she was in a good mood. Later that evening, in a gesture of magnanimity, I invited her criticism.

"Honey, the Bible says that a wise man gets as much criticism as he can. I've been thinking lately that you might be able to help me become a better man. Do I have any blind spots I need to work on?"

Probably wondering what had motivated my question, she replied, "You're already a good man, Robert."

"Yeah, I know that, dear, but there must be some little area where I could improve. Can't you think of anything?"

"Do you really want me to?" she asked enthusiastically.

"Sure," I said, a little annoyed that she was warming to the idea. An hour later, we had covered eight major character flaws, beginning with vanity.

The fact is that you never outgrow your need for discipline. "Without discipline," says Elizabeth Hurlock, "the adolescent will not develop the ego controls needed to help him adjust to the reality demands of life."[2]

Before we evaluate the types of discipline from which the parent of a teenager can choose, let's consider the purpose of discipline.

THE AIM OF DISCIPLINE

If the Apostle Paul had been married with teenagers, he might have escaped with his wife for an extended weekend at the Holidome in Hebron and written a postcard back to his children. It might have started out a lot like Philippians 2:12—"Therefore, my dear teens, as you have always obeyed—not only in my presence, but now much more in my absence. . . ."

What parent would not rejoice in a teen who is the same person when "no one is watching?" The goal of discipline is the self-government of the teenager.

The ultimate test of our disciplinary patterns then, is the degree to which they help our teens grow toward maturity. We want our children not only to be able to make all of their own decisions, but to face the consequences of them, whether good or bad.

THE TYPES OF DISCIPLINE

Kurt Lewin and Diana Baumrind have identified three common types of parental discipline.[3] It may be helpful for you to recognize characteristics of your own disciplinary style and learn the behavior which results from it.

AUTHORITARIAN (THE "IRON ROD")	RESULTS
Selfish, unsympathetic, cold	*Determined rebelliousness*
Harsh and dictatorial	*Broken will*
Magnifies his own authority	*Destroys cheerfulness and ambition*

Partial and impatient	*Pushes teen to destructive behavior*
Unduly severe	*No respect for man's authority or God's authority*
Angry and uncontrolled; Magnifies indiscretion	*Affects nerves of teen*
Publicly exposes and humiliates; Uses force and military control; Gives loud-voiced commands	*Develops a spirit of "I don't care"*

I have counseled many college students who were the products of authoritarian homes and churches. Often they leave home and face a non-legalistic environment which forces them to reach within for a vital faith with which to face the world—and they come up spiritually bankrupt. No one is there to tell them what they must believe. They seem incapable of making crucial decisions or acting for themselves.

Such teens have been so long under the "iron rule" that they have no confidence in their own judgment. They are often easy prey for someone with a stronger will, leading in the wrong direction. They do not have the stability of character to handle negative peer influence.

In his study of teens who have been overdisciplined, Samuel Southard reports a high level of bitterness. Though his study showed that teenagers from authoritarian homes professed respect for their parents, a deeper analysis revealed much buried hostility toward their parents.[4]

As Dudley says, "inside [children raised by authoritarian parents] simmers a hostility that eventually boils over once they are safely out from under the control of the authority figure. Then they may reject the values that they were forced to conform to, or may spend their adult lives going through the motions of morality without any real personal conviction in a sort of mindless goodness."[5]

God did not create the human mind to be under the

complete control of another. By the time children reach their teen years, they should already be learning to think for themselves.

PERMISSIVE "DO AS YOU PLEASE"	RESULTS
Blindly indulges; Allows teen to rule	*Open rebellion; creates stubborn self-will*
Sentimentally wavers; Coaxes and bribes	*Defies authority; uses deceit or evasion to avoid punishment*
Accepts substitute behavior; Unquestioningly submits to will of teen	*Follows his own headstrong, ungoverned will*

Many parents who choose the permissive pattern of discipline doubtlessly do so because they believe it is the "loving" way to raise children. As commendable as their motives might be, their knowledge of human nature is deficient. Before Benjamin Spock penned his non-disciplinary philosophies, Dr. Paul of Tarsus made the following diagnosis of parents and teens alike: "[We] were by nature children of wrath" (Ephesians 2:3b).

When raising teenagers, too little control can be just as bad as too much. When parents do not have the courage to censure wrong in their teen, or if through disinterest or even laziness makes no attempt to keep their family holy before God, they have abdicated their leadership position and will be held accountable for the evil which results from their neglect.

Parents who gratify their teen's every wish are often surprised when that teen shows little respect for them. On the other hand, teenagers whose parents set firm but fair boundaries for them have been known to write letters like this one, shared with me by a grateful mother.

Dear Mom and Dad,

I know that sometimes I act like I'm upset when you want to know where I'm going and what time I'll be home and all that stuff. And I know that I've accused you a lot of being the only parents in this solar system as strict as you are.

But I just wanted you to know that I love you a lot and it makes me feel good to know that you care about me.

Your daughter,

Sheila

AUTHORITATIVE (DEMOCRATIC "LOVING DISCIPLINE")	RESULTS
Self-controlled	*Preserves self-respect*
Shows love and kindness	*Inspires with courage*
Uses great tact and gentleness	*Binds teens' hearts to parents*
Makes friends with the teen; Shows sympathy and understanding	*Obedience from principle,* *not compulsion*
Shows firmness and strict discipline	*Results not apparent at once,* *but develop over a lifetime*
Under God's own discipline	*Leads to self-discipline and* *self-control*

Ephesians 6:4 aptly sums up the authoritative or democratic form of discipline: "And now a word to you parents. Don't keep on scolding and nagging your children, making them angry and resentful. Rather, bring them up with the loving discipline the Lord himself approves, with suggestions and godly advice" (LB).

God has never taken pleasure in forced obedience or blind submission. You must win your teen's affection if you want to impress him with Christian truth. With genuine love and esteem for the dignity of the teen, it is possible for a parent to enlist the will and the reason of a teenager on the side of obedience. When kindness and affection attend them, teenagers respect parents of uniform firmness and unimpassioned control.

As a cause for which teens reject religion, parental style of discipline is closely related to the topic of emancipation from parents. Practical suggestions for both issues will be offered in the next chapter.

CHAPTER
10

When I Want Your Opinion, I'll Give It to You

Reason #8: Struggle for emancipation from parents

"You're never going to get respect from someone who has changed your diapers."

OVERHEARD FROM A NEIGHBORHOOD TEEN

T HE GOAL OF SELF-GOVERNMENT will never be attained until the teenager has negotiated the single most important step from adolescence to adulthood: the transition to healthy independence.

Throughout childhood, the teens have experienced the security and relative ease of being controlled by their parents. Neither their cognitive abilities nor emotional needs have been in conflict with this dependent position. The parents' values, including their religious ones, have been the teens' own. But the time has come for the young people to begin to be their "own persons."

Teens who are lovingly disciplined toward emancipation from parental control have more positive feelings for their families than those who have been severely trained. Robert Grinder reports, "Investigators have confirmed that, on the whole, an adolescent who is granted autonomy by his parents will maintain close relations with them."[1]

Still, it is the rare teen who passes from the dependency of childhood to the independence of adulthood without some measure of trauma. In fact, some teenagers feel that the only way they can achieve their own identity is to reject the values of their parents. Rogers contends that when parents attempt to stamp their values on their adolescent children, thereby frustrating their attainment of self-determination and autonomy, they unconsciously drive them to accept alternative values.[2]

Often teens see their parents as possessors of power upon which they are dependent and at least a part of which they need to possess. If your teenagers sense that they will be unable to attain any control over their own lives, they will become even more aware of their dependency and impotence. Parents with an insidious need for power and control over their teen may have loaded and primed a "charge" during early childhood that will result in an explosion during adolescence.

Narramore relates what can happen if parents try to maintain rigid control. "[Many] teenagers turn against the church as an expression of anger toward their parents. When church life is important to parents, teens know they can irritate or upset us by spurning the thing that is closest to us. In this instance, the church is not the teen's real target."[3]

WHAT'S A PARENT TO DO?

I recently read a poem (written by that prolific author, Anonymous) which reminded me how much parents impact the lives of their teenagers:

I took a piece of plastic clay
And idly fashioned it one day,
And as my fingers pressed it still,
It moved and yielded to my will.

I came again when days were passed;
The bit of clay was hard at last,
The form I gave it still it bore,
But I could change that form no more.
I took a piece of living clay
And touched it gently day by day,
And molded with my power and art
A young child's soft and yielding heart.
I came again when years were gone;
It was a mind I looked upon;
That early impress still he wore,

BUT I COULD CHANGE THAT FORM NO MORE.

The good news is that the clay is not hard yet; there is still time for a teenager's life to be shaped. If the parent is open to a firm, but loving authoritative style of discipline, which has as its aim the self-government of the teen, there are many positive things that can be done to lead to that teen's responsible independence.

Dorothy Rogers insightfully states, "Emancipation is almost as crucial a test for the parent as it is for the adolescent himself. On both sides there should be preparation for the time when the fledgling adult leaves the nest."[4]

Here are some ideas for that time of preparation.

1. Let God's goal for your teen be the same as yours.

". . . until we all become mature, attaining to the whole measure of the fullness of Christ. Then we will no longer be infants" (Ephesians 4:13b, 14a).

The term "adolescence" comes from the Latin word *adolescere,* which means "to grow" or "to grow to maturity." It is God's plan for your teenager to "leave the elementary teachings about Christ and go on to maturity" (Hebrews

6:1). Teens are forced to remain "baby Christians" if there are not clearly defined steps marking the recession of parental authority over them.

David Augsburger tells a provocative parable about a man who arrived in a snowbound city, only to find that none of its inhabitants wore shoes. When he asked someone about a particularly impressive building in the center of town, he heard the proud reply: "That is one of our outstanding shoe manufacturing establishments!"

"A what?" I asked in amazement. "You mean you make shoes there?"

"Well, not exactly," said he, a bit abashed. "We talk about making shoes there, and believe me, we have one of the most brilliant young fellows you have ever heard. . . . Just yesterday he moved the people profoundly with his exposition of the necessity of shoe-wearing. Many broke down and wept. It was really wonderful!"

"But why don't they wear them?" said I insistently.

"Ah, that is a good question," he replied. "Why don't we?"[5]

It is nonsensical to build a shoe factory and then die in the cold from not wearing shoes. Is it any less ridiculous to raise your teenagers in the church and not prepare them to be productive, self-governed Christians?

2. Purpose to mold your teen's will—not to break it.

Of Jesus it was said: "He will not shout or cry out, or raise his voice. . . . A bruised reed he will not break, and a smoldering wick he will not snuff out" (Isaiah 42:2, 3).

Teenagers with spirit do not need to be ridden hard like wild broncos until their spirits are broken and their defiance conquered. In fact, any attempt to "break the will" of a teen is a serious blunder, no matter how good the intentions of the parent. The adolescent's will should be guided or molded, but never disregarded or crushed.

Most teens are going to need all the strength of will they can muster to repel the voices which will call them from the narrow path. Therefore, as the parent of a teen, you should treat his will with tenderness and discretion. The will is a sacred treasure and must not be hammered to pieces by one who should be helping it to grow in the right direction. Be content to allow the circumstances of life to do the hammering while you, the parent, concentrate on the shaping.

3. Teach him to place his will on the side of God's will.

"For it is God who works in you to will and to act according to his good purpose" (Philippians 2:13).

Teens convinced against their will remain unconvinced still. But those who surrender their will to God (not to you) will discover God's perfect plan for them.

The "will" is that governing power in the nature of every person. It is the power of choice and of decision which eventually every teenager must possess.

Teens can no sooner change their own heart than they can control their thoughts or desires. But by purposely placing their will on the side of God's will, teens may stand where nothing can force them to do evil. This is a lesson not easily learned but worth any effort to communicate.

4. Speak with one voice when disciplining.

"Then make my joy complete by being like-minded, having the same love, being one in spirit and purpose" (Philippians 2:2).

Parents who are not united in their family government present their teens with a dilemma. Which voice should they consider and obey? Or would it be better to heed neither and do their own thing? Getting mixed signals from adults is a source of frustration and confusion to a teenager.

One reason that parents often line up on differing sides of a disciplinary issue is very basic: there are usually at least two cogent sides to each issue. For reasons which probably have deep roots in their backgrounds, the parents separately decide upon a measure of discipline. One opts for leniency and pleads a case built on mercy, forgiveness, and longsuffering love. The other chooses severe punishment and calls on the need for justice, retribution, and tough love.

The real need is for parents to come together and learn to make a joint decision in that area of tension which exists between the opposing sides. I have learned from years of counseling and being counseled that the mind of Christ is usually well-informed by both sides of an issue. "[In Christ] mercy and truth have met together. Grim justice and peace have kissed!" (Psalm 85:10, LB)

5. *And when you speak, keep your tongue from evil.*

"A gentle answer turns away wrath, but a harsh word stirs up anger" (Proverbs 15:1).

Most of the words which surface at the moment you feel betrayed by, disappointed in, or angry with your teen are far better left unsaid. Irreparable damage has been done to parent/teen relationships by thoughtless statements that, once blurted, began their poisonous path deep into the teenage psyche.

> *You're never going to amount to anything!*
> *Hey, stupid, don't you know how to listen?*
> *You've never been anything but an embarrassment to me.*
> *I wish you'd never been born!*

Paul gave us good advice in Ephesians 4:29 for the way to reprove our teens: "Do not let any unwholesome talk come out of your mouths, but only what is helpful for building others up according to their needs, that it may benefit those who listen."

6. *Be persistent—never give up.*

"And let us not get tired of doing what is right, for after

a while we will reap a harvest of blessing if we don't get discouraged and give up" (Galatians 6:9, LB).

Even with your best efforts to prepare your teen for self-government, there likely will be times when you experience setbacks:

"Hey, Dad!" the teenager shouted. "I finally raised that twenty dollars I've needed for so long."

"Good work, son. Any young man worth his salt should do everything he can to make himself independent of his father and learn to stand on his own two feet. How did you do it?"

"I borrowed it from Mom."

Seriously, teens are not the only ones who experience frustration and discouragement. Parenting a teenager can drain your emotional reservoir and leave you battling anxiety and depression. In fact, such was the case for me a few years ago during a series of meetings I was preaching in Illinois.

The family with whom I was staying turned over their teenage son's lair to me for the week. As I lay on my back on his attic room bed, I grew even more disconsolate, pondering a problem for which I could see no chance for resolution. It was then that my eyes focused on a poster mounted over the bed. A picture of a dejected high school football player with a battle-worn helmet in his lap and tears in his eyes was framed by the words "*I quit!*"

I thought to myself, "I can relate!" But as I studied the poster I noticed in the bottom right-hand corner a tiny drawing of a craggy hill with a cross on top of it, underscored by the words, "I didn't."

In the course of parenting an adolescent, times of discouragement may come. But the time for giving up on your teen never will. It is never "checkmate" when the King has another move!

7. *Have few rules and enforce them.*

"Take my yoke upon you and learn from me, for I am

gentle and humble in heart, and you will find rest for your souls. For my yoke is easy and my burden is light" (Matthew 11:29, 30).

It has been said of Jesus that His skill for making the best fitting yokes in Galilee was renowned, and over His carpenter's shop door was a sign, "My Yokes Are Easy." The slogan need not change for disciplining teens. The rules should be few and clear enough that they can be understood by the teen and firmly enforced by the parent.

Adolescents have minds that can reason from cause to effect, and most of them appreciate an adult who is willing to explain the reasons behind the rules. And when rules are being drawn up, it should be remembered that teenagers have the right not only to voice their own opinions but to contribute toward establishing their own limitations. The teen who has a real say in setting up his boundaries is more likely to stay within them.

8. *Do not smooth over your teen's opportunity to suffer the consequences of his mistakes.*

"We also rejoice in our sufferings, because we know that suffering produces perseverance, and perseverance, character" (Romans 5:3b, 4).

There is always the temptation for an empathic parent to protect his teen from adversity.

> *Your coach is really a jerk. Just because you missed a practice is no reason for you to sit on the bench for a whole game.*

> *The teachers at your school are so unfair, dear. They have no right to give you such hard examinations.*

> *It wasn't your fault, son. She should have told you she was off her birth control pills.*

> *Your youth pastor is asking too much of you. I mean, nobody's perfect.*

For whatever the reason, encouraging teenagers to avoid suffering steals from them the only path to proven character and usually fosters self-pity. On the contrary, as other-worldly as it sounds, it would be wiser to teach them to "consider it pure joy whenever you face trials of many kinds" (James 1:2).

9. Direct your teen to the source of pardon and power.

"Now this is eternal life: that they may know you, the only true God, and Jesus Christ, whom you have sent" (John 17:3).

There are those rare, lucid moments when you get a brief but penetrating look at the very reason for your existence; a glimpse of the *summum bonum* of life—like C. S. Lewis' heroine in *That Hideous Strength,* when she suddenly realized that the belief in God she had rejected as a young woman was actually true: "The world had already turned out to be so very unlike what she had expected. There might be a life after death: a Heaven: a Hell: God. The thought glowed in her mind for a second like a spark that has fallen on shavings and then a second later, like those shavings, her whole mind was in a blaze—or with just enough left outside the blaze to utter some kind of protest. 'But . . . but this is unbearable. I ought to have been told.' "[6]

There is nothing more crucial for a teenager than to have a salvation experience with the Lord Jesus. Your teens should not reach the end of their days and be able to say, "But this is unbearable. I ought to have been told."

Sitting with my wife in a large audience at a Christian college one evening, I heard Jim Dobson ask the question, "Where is a relay race won, anyway?"

Having "run track" for years, I thought I knew the answer, but I wasn't sure what point he was trying to make.

"A relay race is won or lost," he continued, "by the passing of the baton. The team that is best at passing the baton will be the winner. For your families, that baton is knowing Jesus Christ as Lord and Savior."

Dobson was right. It doesn't matter how fast your teen runs the race of life. Sure, you may have bragging rights in the neighborhood for a few days if he scores the winning touchdown, or she is elected homecoming queen. But is there anything more important than their secure grasp of The Baton?

Modern psychology tells us that it can be harmful to be an only child, detrimental to be the youngest, damaging to be in the middle, and undesirable to be the oldest. There seems no way out, except to be born an adult. And since that is impossible, perhaps we can begin treating our teens a little more as if they were adults. When their behavior doesn't seem to merit such respect, avoid the temptation to threaten, argue, humiliate, compare, or challenge them to rebel. Somewhere in the tension between God's mercy and justice, you will find the Mind of Christ.

Achieving independence from parents is essential for the teenager. It is not unusual that rebellion against parents who do not encourage the emancipation of their teen is often accompanied by alienation from the religion of those parents.

CHAPTER
11

"Unmoved Mover" or Friend?

Reason #9: Negative concept of religion

"When you think of Jesus Christ, you should say 'What a man!' But we usually make Him too sissified when we think and talk about Him. Those hardened fishermen would never have followed Him if He had been a pansy."—DAVID HUBBARD

ONE REASON THAT CHRISTIAN teens are leaving the church stems from their fallacious concept of what Christianity is all about. Just who is Jesus Christ, and how do you relate to Him? To most church-related teenagers, Jesus is a shadowy figure whom they heard about around a campfire, in an austere worship service, or in someone else's testimony.

My teenage perception of Jesus was no one I wanted to introduce to the guys on the track team, because He probably couldn't run the mile under ten minutes. In fact, because of my erroneous image of the person of Jesus Christ, my association with Christianity was more of an embarrassment to me during high school than it was an inspiration.

At the root of my decision to become a Christian was the discovery that the image of Christ I grew up with was very unlike the one that surges from the pages of the New Testament. The Gospel of John reveals that the moral injustices of the money-changers galvanized an athletic young prophet into action one memorable day in the Temple. As Bruce Barton describes it: "There was in his eyes a flaming moral purpose. As His right arm rose and fell, striking its blows with that little whip, the sleeve dropped back to reveal muscles hard as iron."[1]

Much of my new concept of Christ began on my first trip to Israel. To kick a rock down the same dusty street that He traveled in Nazareth; to skip a flat stone on the Sea of Galilee and picture Him as an eight-year-old; to gaze at the "Place of the Skull" and visualize the Crucifixion; to watch a tourist emerge from the Garden Tomb and feel the excitement and reality of the Resurrection; these scenes were real faith-builders for me. But the greatest impact came on the day our tour guide approached me and said, "Mr. Bob, what will you do on your free day tomorrow?"

"I'm not sure, Moishe. I think I'll run from Jerusalem to Emmaus."

"No, Mr. Bob!" he shouted. "You must not do such a foolish thing. You will die!"

"Moishe, I checked it out. It's less than ten miles, and back in the States people are running marathons of over twenty-six miles all the time. I know I can make it."

"But the way to Emmaus is through the mountains of the Judean wilderness. You must take the old Roman road. Two Olympic runners tried to make it years ago. We never heard from them again."

He was obviously sincere, and I didn't want to offend him, but I had to tell him the reason I chose that destination in the first place. "Moishe, I'm positive that Jesus Christ made that same trip. In fact, I've got a painting back home called 'The Road to Emmaus' that shows Him with two of his disciples. Jesus used to do that kind of thing all the time."

Spontaneously, Moishe, an Israeli army captain when he wasn't leading tours, shot back, "Well then, Mr. Bob. This

Jesus of yours, he must have been . . . some kind of guy!"

Even after beginning to understand the authentic Jesus of the New Testament, many teenagers still do not know how to make a connection with Him. Youth who are not certain about their relationship with God exhibit two fundamental problems.

The first is a sense of isolation from others. They inhibit their emotions and tend to act in control. They grow increasingly self-centered, resulting in an inflated opinion of their own importance.

The second problem is revealed by a sense of anomie, a feeling that life has no meaning. Speaking of their confused relationship with God, Merton Strommen disclosed that many of the teens in his study believed that salvation by works was the theology of the church, and they admitted that they had no personal experience of God's grace in their lives.[2]

I found a similar situation in my own survey. Among youth in the study who showed a general alienation from religion, the typical responses were as follows:

"God loves me more when I've been doing right than when I've given in to temptation." (agree)

"The way to be accepted by God is to try sincerely to live a good life." (agree)

"I don't have much of a chance of being saved because the requirements are too strict." (strongly agree)

"The main emphasis of the Gospel is on God's rules for right living." (agree)

Teenagers in the church who understand that Christianity consists of a personal relationship with God in Jesus Christ are far more likely to be positive about the church than those who believe religion consists of earning God's favor by their performance.

WHAT'S A PARENT TO DO?

In communicating a true concept of Christianity to a teenager, a parent's wisest course would be to take Paul's advice in Ephesians 5:1. "Follow God's example in everything you do just as a much loved child imitates his father" (LB).

Our objective, then, is to discover what God's example for parents of teenagers is.

1. Be a touchable parent.

"But while he was still a long way off, his father saw him and was filled with compassion for him; he ran to his son, threw his arms around him and kissed him" (Luke 15:20).

Mark gives us a touching glimpse of Jesus. It is a story which is particularly relevant in a day when an unfortunate school child who contracts the AIDS virus during a blood transfusion is thereafter treated as a social pariah.

Mark tells of a desperate man with leprosy who breaks the law by approaching Jesus and begging Him on his knees.

"If You are willing," he cries, "You can make me clean."

It struck me as odd while reading this story that the leper phrased his question in that manner. My first instinct would have been to plead, "If you can heal me, do it now!"

It must be that the leper knew Jesus was able to heal him; he just doubted that He would. The man was an outcast, an untouchable, a miserable fugitive who was required to announce his own presence with the clapping of boards and the pitiful cry, "Unclean!" It was as if he were saying, "Jesus, I don't doubt Your capacity to heal me—I only doubt Your compassion."

The next words are some of the most sublime in all of Scripture: "Filled with compassion, Jesus reached out his hand and touched the man. 'I am willing,' he said."

You may have a cultural bias against any display of physical affection toward your teen. Your parents seldom embraced you, and it is only natural for you to keep your own distance emotionally from your family. Or perhaps you are just not the impulsive type. You pride yourself on being able to control your feelings. Gushing people annoy you, and hugging is simply too maudlin for your style. For whatever reason you distance yourself from others, you somehow must deal with a God who seems to give a high profile both to touching and being touched.

"Then the Lord reached out his hand and touched my mouth" (Jeremiah 1:9).

"He touches the mountains and they smoke" (Psalm 104:32b).

"For he had healed many, so that those with diseases were pushing forward to touch him" (Mark 3:10).

"Jesus came and touched them. . . ." (Matthew 17:7).

"As many as touched Him were made whole" (Mark 6:56).

Dr. David Bresler, director of Pain Control at UCLA, says, "I often tell my patients to use hugging as part of their treatment for pain. To be held is enormously therapeutic."[3] Researchers have discovered that hugging can help you to live longer, protect you against illness, cure depression and stress, strengthen family relationships, and even help you sleep without pills.

"When a person is touched, the amount of hemoglobin in their blood increases significantly," says Helen Colton, author of *The Joy of Touching*. She adds, "Hemoglobin is a part of the blood that carries vital supplies of oxygen to all organs of the body—including the heart and brain. An increase in hemoglobin tones up the whole body, helps prevent disease and speeds recovery from illness. My fifteen years of research have convinced me that regular hugging can actually prolong life by curing harmful depression and stimulating a strong will to live."[4]

Granted, there are teens who act like they would rather

clean up their bedrooms than be kissed or hugged by a parent. It is only natural at times for your teenagers to need their space, and you can graciously give it to them. But your teens' "touchability" is not the issue. When they need a godly embrace from you, are you available?

2. Be a "friendly" parent.

"I no longer call you servants, for a master doesn't confide in his servants; now you are my friends" (John 15:15).

We serve a God who puts a premium on friendship.

"Abraham believed God . . . and he was called God's friend." (James 2:23).

"The Lord would speak to Moses face to face, as a man speaks with his friend" (Exodus 33:11a).

"The Son of Man . . . a friend of tax collectors and 'sinners' " (Matthew 11:19).

Still, there are those who feel it is not appropriate to be both parent and friend to a teenager. Their rationale goes like this: "It's impossible to maintain discipline if you're too chummy with an adolescent" or "My teenager would lose respect for me if he got to know me on a friendship level."

But if God, Who created us, knows all about us, and disciplines us daily, still finds us worthy enough to seek out our friendship, then maybe we can find a way to make some "friendly" overtures to our teens.

If you are anything like I am, then the experience of "being a friend" does not come naturally to you. In the crucial early years, when I should have been learning how to form give-and-take relationships, I was not a Christian. Consequently, my relational emphases were largely on the "take" side, and even then, I usually only took from others what I felt I had rightfully earned—or just enough so that I wouldn't be in anyone's debt.

That pattern of being emotionally reserved and selfish has

been known to surface in my life as a Christian father and husband. Too often, my own agenda and immediate needs have been more important to me than those of my own family. Besides, it is so much easier for some of us fathers to bury ourselves in our work than to risk exposing ourselves and genuinely befriending the members of our families.

If you are relatively new at being a friend, I am convinced that God would have you start at your home address. You might be surprised by the friendships that await you in your own family.

3. *Cultivate your sense of humor.*

"What has happened to all your joy?" (Galatians 4:15a).

In *The Prophet*, Kahlil Gibran says, "And in the sweetness of friendship let there be laughter and the sharing of pleasures."[5] There are few things which will attract a teenager like laughter. Sometimes we take ourselves so seriously that it is easy to forget we serve a God who values laughter and rejoicing—especially in the midst of suffering.

> *"Consider it pure joy . . . whenever you face trials"* *(James 1:2).*

> *"In this you greatly rejoice, though you may have to suffer"* *(1 Peter 1:6).*

Strommen says that one of the five cries of youth is joy.[6] Teenagers love to laugh and are drawn to celebrations of life. Both the home and church can plug into that theme without secularizing it. There is great power in joy, and who has more of a right to experience it than someone whose sins have been forgiven while receiving ultimate purpose in life? Many teens in my study confirmed Strommen's observation:

> *I feel happy because I know that I am a Christian!*

> *I feel excitement and relief knowing that God is with me, joy knowing that I'm going to heaven, happiness knowing that I'm forgiven.*

131

I'm excited and want to take part in any way I can.

Swimming pools, wide-screen TVs, video games, and exercise equipment might make your home a more "fun place" to be for your teen and his friends. But material trappings matter little if you're not much of a "fun person" to be around. We parents would do well to remember that "the joy of the Lord is our strength" (Nehemiah 8:10).

A FATHER-GOD ANY TEEN WOULD LOVE

"Lord, show us the Father," said Philip to Jesus, "and that will be enough for us." I believe that most teenagers, like Philip, would find it "enough" for them to decide for Christ if we could just show them the Father.

I have always had a special love for my niece, Julie. So when Uncle Sam shipped her father out to the Pacific for a six-month tour of duty, I felt it would be an opportune occasion to spend some time with her.

She was excited but cautious the day we took her to the YMCA to go swimming. She made a point of expressing her fear of going too deep because she didn't know how to swim yet. I saw my chance to build the confidence of this impressionable seven-year-old.

We spent the first half hour in the shallow end of the pool. Naturally athletic, she took to the water like a fish. In a matter of minutes, I pulled my arms from beneath her and she was swimming by herself. Her confidence level was soaring when we took a break and I lifted her onto the pool's edge.

Suddenly the antics at the deep end caught her full attention. Most of the divers were teenage boys doing one and a half gainers onto their faces or "can-openers" to see how much water they could remove from the pool. Seeing her wide-eyed interest, I acted on an impulse.

"You know something, Julie? You could do that. You could jump off that diving board."

"Oh, no, Uncle Bobby! I could never do that!"

"Sure you could, honey. You swim well enough right now that if I helped you, you could do it. No problem. I'll be right under the board to catch you."

She was braver than I thought, and before I knew it I was treading water in the deep end as she stood above me on the diving board. With her toes curled around the front of the board, she looked down at me, and I could see that fear was making its play for her. It was now or never.

"Okay, Julie. Let's go, baby! Jump to Uncle Bobby!"

She was suddenly aware that all eyes were on her. She scanned the crowd and whispered down to me, "I don't think I can do it, Uncle Bobby!"

"Yes, you can," I coaxed. "Right now! Jump to Uncle Bobby!"

I saw fear win out and was sorry that I had pushed her too quickly.

"It's okay, Julie. We'll try another time!"

She carefully backed down the ladder while my wife enveloped her with a towel and some words of encouragement. Just as I was about to leave the deep end, my three-year-old, Joy, arrested me with a commanding shout.

"Hey, Daddy! Stay right there!"

I was so surprised that it didn't cross my mind to stop her. She raced up the ladder, made certain that everyone was watching, marched proudly to the end of the board, and asked if I was ready.

"Sure, Joy. I'm ready. Jump to Daddy!"

With no hesitation, she launched her chubbiness through the air, legs pumping like pistons, and into the water. I was still in such shock that I forgot to catch her! But when her little head bobbed up, she was whooping.

"Oh, Daddy. Let's do it again!"

And this is the Good News for you and your teenager: God's not your uncle. He's your Daddy.

"And so we should not be like cringing, fearful slaves, but we should behave like God's very own children, adopted into the bosom of his family, and calling to him, 'Father, Father' " (Romans 8:15, LB).

He's your touchable, friendly, joy-filled, compassionate Father. Our teenagers do not have to perform to get His attention. Our mutual sin has already accomplished that. Neither do they have to obey to merit His love. He loves them—because HE LOVES THEM, and the Cross is proof enough of that.

If we parents could better show our teens who He is, the chances of their deciding for Christianity would be greater.

CHAPTER
12

God Still Makes House Calls

Reason #10: Lack of family harmony

P ERHAPS YOU'VE SEEN ONE. But if you haven't, you are not alone. There just aren't as many around as there used to be. I've heard it told that years ago, you could find one on almost every farm—but that was before the fast pace of modern living crowded most of them out. Now they seem to be on the verge of extinction. . . .

If you saw one, you would not forget the experience. It would probably smile at you with an affection so guileless you might mistake it for a simple creature without a care in the world. But a closer examination would reveal profound depth and a countenance etched by great joy as well as immeasurable sorrow. You would sense that it had passed through countless valleys and scaled many mountains, and now stood ready for either.

You might be interested to know that there have been occasions when it has flown; but one would hardly call it flighty. It has the capability of attaining great speeds but, unlike most of us, it knows when to slow down and enjoy life. It has learned the art of walking, taking life one day at a time, forgetting yesterday and letting tomorrow worry about itself.

What does it look like? That's hard to say. Sometimes it resembles the father of a teenager when he sets aside time just to take his son for a long walk and find out what's going on inside him. At other times it is the very image of a mother tucking her little girl in, listening to her prayers, and kissing her goodnight. And on very rare occasions, it has been known to conform to the likeness of a brother or sister who shares a couple of cookies or a prized toy.

But you can be sure of one thing: its arms are always open, ready to take another into the warmth and security of its love. It really is a rather remarkable species. In fact, it is God's finest creation. It is *Christianus famelia*—the Christian family.

One of the first steps in preserving any endangered species is to understand the factors which are leading to its extinction. Urie Brofenbrenner offers some insight, suggesting that the origins of teenage alienation lie in the evolution of the American family—especially as the changes isolate teens from their parents and the adult world in general. He cites the following characteristics of the down-ward spiral in family togetherness:

1. *Fathers' vocational choices which remove them from the home for lengthy periods of time.*

2. *An increase in the number of working mothers.*

3. *A critical escalation in the divorce rate.*

4. *A rapid increase in single-parent families.*

5. *A steady decline in the extended family.*

6. *The evolution of the physical environment of the home (family rooms, playrooms, master bedrooms).*

7. *The replacement of the adult by the peer group.*

8. *The isolation of children from the work world.*

9. *The insulation of schools from the rest of society (which, according to Brofenbrenner, has caused the schools to become "one of the most potent breeding grounds for alienation in American society.")*[1]

In my study, a lack of harmony in the home was positively correlated with teenagers feeling alienated from the church. Teens who showed an across-the-board alienation from religion responded as follows to these statements:

"There are many conflicts and arguments in our family." (agree)

"In our family we respect each other's privacy." (disagree)

"Our family members are critical of each other." (agree)

"We do not forgive each other easily in our family." (agree)

"The members of our family hardly ever hurt each other's feelings." (disagree)

RATING YOUR FAMILY

The recreational sex and anti-family mentalities that characterize our society have led to epidemic divorce rates and threaten to ravage the moral fabric of our teens. But there are two major reasons we still have hope: a long-suffering God and the Christian home.

There are certain tenets which seem to undergird every godly family. Pulling together some of the principles I've already discussed in this book, I offer you and your teen the opportunity to rate your own family experience. Examine each of these principles, using them as mirrors to evaluate your own situation.

You might want to plan a special family evening some time this week to answer the questions that accompany each of these principles and discuss them. Check the ones which your family agrees need the most work. You might want to rank your "top ten," with number 1 representing the principle needing the most improvement in your household.

ACCEPTANCE

"Accept one another, then, just as Christ accepted you" (Romans 15:7).

One of the world's most subtle ploys to fashion our defeat is to label and limit us by our differences. At home, school, or in the church, you might hear "He's sure not as smart as his brother," or "She's the homely one in the family."

In the Christian home, however, you should be accepted no matter who you are or what you look like. Certainly one reason God has given us the family is to provide a place in the universe where you are loved "in spite of—."

While the world employs every conceivable scheme to dehumanize us, the family can fight back through the mutual encouragement of its members. It is an environment in which we can build up one another's self-esteem.

Questions:

1. *Does your family play favorites with certain members?*

2. *Is there unhealthy competition among individuals in the family?*

3. *Do you feel that you are accepted for who you are, and encouraged by your family?*

LOVE

"Keep yourselves in the love of God" (Jude 21a).

I once asked two gentlemen in the hallway of a church if I could borrow a comb. Instinctively, they checked their back pockets, and then looked at each other and burst into laughter. They were both bald as cucumbers! I felt foolish, but I learned a lesson. Never go to a bald-headed man if you need a comb.

In the same respect, there are certain places you avoid when you are looking for love. God has given us only two contexts in which to experience real love: the church and the family. When you don't get enough love at home, sometimes it takes forever to understand what that word means at church. By then it is often too late; you have lost your family.

Questions:

4. *Have you said, "I love you" to your teen/parent today?*

5. *Is your family open about showing love to one another?*

6. *If not, what are some ways you can start being more of a loving family?*

SACRIFICE

"But in humility consider others better than yourselves" (Philippians 2:3b).

There are several different types of love that can be found in the Biblical saga of King David:

PHILEO—the kind of "friendship love" that characterized David's relationship with Jonathan.

EROS—the "sexual love" that attracted him to Bathsheba and led to Uriah's death.

STORGE—the "familial love" that David had for Absalom, a love which broke his heart when his son rebelled.

All of these types of love were "natural" for David, in that they were instinctive and did not require any great inner struggle on his part to maintain. But there was a love in David's life that was very unnatural. It surfaced after *the sin* and crushed the pride of the wayward king.

Though David knew that his death would be too great a punishment for his offenses, God had already made him a promise: My love will never be taken away from [you], as I took it from Saul, whom I removed before you. Your house and your kingdom will endure forever before me" (II Samuel 7:15, 16).

This "supernatural" type of love is *agape,* and can perhaps best be understood as "love measured by sacrifice." It marks the supreme distinction of the Christian home.

There have been many times in our marriage when I've noticed my wife go without something so that our children could have what they needed. When questioned about the low regard she has for her own needs, she sincerely sees no problem and harbors no resentment. On the contrary, she communicates a sense of joy in her sacrifice. That is "agape" in action.

Sacrificing is perhaps the most difficult of all the principles to apply to the family, because it goes directly against the egotistical bent of our human nature. I want to watch my favorite television programs. I want to eat my favorite foods at mealtime. I want to talk about what I did today, and so on.

Questions:

7. *Do you resent making sacrifices for the members of your family?*

8. *What would you consider giving up to help a family member?*

RIGHT PRIORITIES

"But seek first the Kingdom of God" (Matthew 6:33).

I've heard the word *joy* used as an acronym to express correct priorities: Jesus first, Others second, and You third. It is not difficult to recognize what is most important to your family members, parents or teens—just observe what they spend their time, money, and affection on. Jesus said, "For where your treasure is, there your heart will be also" (Matthew 6:21).

There is nothing innately evil about most of our avocations. But there is something wrong when we give more energy to our hobbies than we do to our relationships with God and each other.

Questions:

9. *Is it your family's main goal for each member to grow as Christians?*

10. *What are some ways you could prioritize your life and help that goal to be realized?*

DISCIPLINE

"He who ignores discipline comes to shame" (Proverbs 13:18a).

I went to a church youth party at someone's home recently and was greeted at the door by about twenty-five pairs of shoes. I stepped over the aromatic pile and strolled into the kitchen, but I didn't get far before a resident teenager confronted me.

Tactfully she said, "Uh, Bob, I know we all run the risk of getting the Bubonic plague, but could you please take off your shoes, too? Sorry, but it's a house rule."

The first thing I thought about was the holes in my socks. The second was how refreshing it was to hear a teen in a home, in the absence of her parents, uphold the "house rules." It was obviously not just her parents' house or her parents' rules. She had an investment in this home, also, and cared about its proper functioning. She knew that it takes discipline to make it work.

Questions:

11. *Are the rules in your house fair and scriptural?*

12. *Do you feel there are too many rules in your family? not enough rules?*

13. *Do your teens have a say in making those rules?*

14. *Is there room for forgiveness when a rule is inadvertently broken?*

15. *Does each member of the family do his best to see that the rules are kept?*

COMMUNICATION

"Speak to one another . . ." (Ephesians 5:19).

The story is told of a crusty farmer and his taciturn wife who were eating a meal in silence at their kitchen table. Suddenly a cyclone invaded their farm, tore the roof off the house, lifted them up with their table and chairs, and set them down intact in the middle of the barnyard before roaring on its way.

The farmer noticed his wife sitting at the table weeping, and said, "Aw, Ethel, quit your crying. You ain't hurt!"

"I'm not crying because I'm hurt," she replied. "I'm crying because this is the first time we've eaten out in fifteen years!"

It's remarkable how long we can go without communicating our innermost feelings with one another. If there is one problem that most families suffer from, it is certainly the lack of quality communication. Family members spin in their separate orbits, occasionally making a re-entry just long enough to sit down for a meal. It is a constant source of amazement to me that people living under the same roof for years can end up hardly knowing each other and seldom comprehending why they behave as they do.

Questions:

16. *Do you feel free to "open up" in your family?*

17. *Do you really listen when someone in your family tries to share something he or she feels is important?*

18. *Do you feel that others listen to you?*

FAITH

"The prayer of a righteous man is powerful and effective" (James 5:16b).

In the dramatic story of Elijah on Mount Carmel (I Kings 18), there is a statement which serves as an eloquent commentary on one of the reasons teenagers reject religion. Striving to invoke fire upon their sacrifice, the prophets of

Baal performed their frantic religious rituals for hours, only to see no action from their god. The sentence which follows their futile worship is this: "But there was no response, no one answered, [therefore] no one paid attention."

Before we can expect them to pay attention, we need to show our teens that we believe in a God of power and life.

One of the wiser things parents of teens can do is to open their home to other enthusiastic Christians for Bible studies, weekend visits, or just for dinner now and then. I have noticed a "spiritual osmosis" effect take place when my teenagers spend time with Christian guests in our home.

Questions:

19. *Is there a sense of God's aliveness in your family?*

20. *Does God affect your everyday lives, or do you think about Him mostly on Sundays?*

As you and your teens continue to grow together, your answer to these questions might change significantly. Try this exercise again in six months, and see how far you've come!

CHAPTER
13

Tearing Down the Walls

Many family counselors cite a simple lack of understanding between parents and teens as the major reason for the generation gap. Expecting parents to understand their teenagers may be as unrealistic as expecting your teen to put gas in the family car. No matter how hard you try or how many books you read on adolescent psychology, your own teens will, in many ways, remain a mystery to you.

You will never understand, for example, how your teen can break his school record in the hundred meter dash when his time from the breakfast table to the lawn mower could be measured with a sundial.

You will be mystified that your teen can spend two hours on the phone covering every imaginable subject and then come up mute during family devotions.

The riddle of the Sphinx is easier to decipher than observing teens who can get up at 5 A.M. to jog eight miles, lift weights for two hours every evening, never miss a chance to steal a base, make a lay-up, or catch a pass . . . yet need to be driven to the garbage can.

Still, whether we understand each other or not, the generation gap can be spanned. God has a good track record for removing barriers and reconciling His children to one another. There is no reason for the parent/teen years to be characterized by rebellion and mutual hostility. I am convinced that by the time you have weathered pierced ears and paper routes, driver's training and dating anxiety, Sunday morning battles for the bathroom and Sunday night term papers, you and your high-school graduate can part as friends who want to see each other again as often as possible. Paul wrote to the Ephesians,

> *"For he himself is our peace, who has made the two one and has destroyed the barrier, the dividing wall of hostility. . . . His purpose was to create in himself one new man out of the two, thus making peace, and in this one body to reconcile both of them to God through the cross, by which he put to death their hostility."* (Ephesians 2:14, 15)

This book has focused on many ways to tear down the walls that naturally arise between most parents and their teens. As a fellow parent of teenagers, I have encouraged you often to "follow God's example in everything you do, just as a much-loved child imitates his father" (Ephesians 5:1, LB). I believe a final look at His example would serve as a good summary.

PARENTING A TEEN IS NOT YOUR JOB

On my son's fifth birthday, he received an inordinate amount of presents and attention from his friends, neighbors, and relatives. He was the focal point of a large party and he was enjoying every moment of it. Showing off for about a dozen of his playmates, he fell off his new bike and skinned his knees on the driveway. Picking him up quickly, I shut off his tears by reminding him of all the gifts that awaited him inside the house. That evening when I was tucking him in bed following our nightly wrestling match/pillow fight, it occurred to me that he had been doted on so much this birthday that his head might benefit from a little deflating. Acting on an impulse I asked,

"Son, you think your friends really love you, don't you?"

"Well, sure, Dad!" came his confident reply.

"And you think your Grandma and Grandpa love you, too, don't you?"

"Sure, Dad! Did you see that bike they gave me?"

"And son, you think that I really love you, don't you?"

"Sure, Dad!" came the expected answer.

"Well, son," I said with the tongue firmly planted in my cheek. "I don't love you. I don't love you at all."

As soon as those words escaped my lips, I wished that I had not said them. At first, his little face screwed up in confusion, and I thought he might cry. To my relief though, his frown was replaced by a smile, and he blurted out,

"Oh, yes, you do!"

"You're right! But how do you know that I love you?" I queried.

He thought for a moment and answered, "Because you got me a present too!"

"OK, but how else do you know that I love you?"

Searching his mind, he replied, "Because you wrestle with me, Dad!"

"That's great, son, but isn't there any other reason for you to know that I love you?"

The silence in the darkness of his bedroom was soon broken with a cry of, "That's easy, Dad! Today when I fell down, you were there to pick me up!"

When I shared this story with my wife, two key truths

occurred to us. First, when we do something right in raising our children, we are most likely imitating the example that God the Father has given us. And secondly, in the best ways that we parents show love to our children, so our Heavenly Father cares for us. These truths should be particularly encouraging to the parents of teenagers.

The reason we are even able to follow His example in relating to our teens is not because of our own abilities as parents, but because He is at work within us. "For it is God who works in you to will and to act according to his good purpose" (Philippians 2:13).

Only three persons have ever been able to live the Christian life, let alone successfully raise Christian teenagers: God the Father, Christ the Son, and the Holy Spirit—and they dwell within you (Colossians 2:9, 10) for that purpose. Your ultimate responsibility is to receive the forgiveness afforded you by the death of our Lord Jesus via personal repentance, begin parenting in the power of the Holy Spirit, and leave the results up to God. For you, a Christian parent, to live is Christ, not Christ-like (Philippians 1:21).

It is as self-defeating as it is unscriptural for you to whip yourself into a frenzy of guilt over your failures as a parent. The only unscarred experts on teenagers never had any. The only parent who made no mistakes raising his teen was God—and He loves you: "Cast all your anxiety on Him, for He cares for you" (I Peter 5:7).

WHAT IF GOD TOLD YOU HE DIDN'T LOVE YOU?

What if tonight in a bad dream you saw God sitting on His throne reading a scroll entitled, "Parents Who Have Blown It with Their Teen?" His eyes scan the lists, past the Hefners, the Hitlers and the Huxleys, until they come to rest on your name. God looks up and says to you, "I don't love you. I don't love you at all."

Such a scene would not only be a nightmare, it would be

a lie. "Oh, yes, you do!" you would cry. "I know that you love me—for three reasons!"

1. *"Because You gave me a present, God. No one ever loved me enough to give me what You have."*

The magnitude of His gift to us parents became more vivid to me a few years ago at the funeral of the wife of one of my best friends. At age thirty-one, with a five-year-old and a two-year-old down the hall and her baby of four weeks in the room next door, Karen accidentally electrocuted herself with her hairdryer in the bathroom. Three days later at the memorial service I listened as her pastor read notes that she had written in the margins of her Bible. After a few moments, he felt compelled to stop reading and joined his congregation in a poignant time of weeping.

Through my own tears, I glanced around the church and realized that everyone was crying. I had never experienced corporate grief like that before. "Why," I wondered, "is this funeral so much harder than any other I've ever attended?"

The answer came to me later that day after Karen's husband movingly observed, "She lived long enough for so many people to get to know her and love her, and yet she had so many years ahead of her to live. She was cut down in the middle of her life."

"Cut down in the middle of life"—that phrase surfaced again in the car trip home from the funeral when I realized that it also described the death of Jesus Christ. He lived long enough to endear Himself to thousands, yet had a lifetime of memories ahead. When He was agonizing in the Garden the night before His death and asking, "Father, if you are willing, take this cup from me" (Luke 22:42), might He not have been thinking, "There is so much left to do. There are so many lepers still to be touched, Pharisees who remain unconvinced, tax-collectors to be saved, families to be restored, and children to be embraced. There is so much more life to be lived."

It was because He loved you and me that He finished His prayer with, ". . . yet not my will, but yours be done," and went out to be cut down in the middle of His life—for the sins of the parents and teenagers of that day as well.

It is because you are much-loved by God and worth the death of Jesus Christ that you can love your teenagers through their rebellion without feeling that you must win the parent/teen conflicts. Most Christian parents are aware of John 3:16 ("For God so loved the world that He gave. . . ."), but few are aware of I John 3:16: "This is how we know what love is: Jesus Christ laid down his life for us. And so we ought to lay down our lives for our brothers."

What would Karen have given to have the chance to see her babies grow to maturity—to know her children as teenagers and friends? Cut down in the middle of life. There is a harder fate than raising teens.

"Yes, You could tell me that You don't love me, but I know that You do because,

2. *You wrestle with me, God. You didn't gift me with parenting and then leave me to my own devices. You are in my world and actively care about the most mundane of my parental responsibilities. I can make it because I know You will live up to Your name, Immanuel, 'God with us.'* "

Shortly after the premature death of our third child, my wife and I were commiserating with each other while reading the beloved Shepherd's Psalm. Fighting deep despair, we were looking for help from Scripture in dealing with the pain of separation. Joyce noticed a significant word in a well-known passage. "Yea, though I walk through the valley of the shadow of death," she read. "Robert, I believe this is God's word to us. We are going to get through this together."

Then I recognized the reason we were going to make it through this ordeal together: ". . . for Thou art with me." The central glory of the gospel and the good news for us as the parents of teenagers is that "The tabernacle of God is among men" (Revelation 21:3). When John wrote, "The Word became flesh and dwelt among us," he used a remarkable word which can be translated, "pitched His tent" among us. God has moved in for the duration. You are not parenting alone, even if you are a single parent. His promise is still true: "Never will I leave you; never will I forsake you" (Hebrews 13:5b).

"You could tell me that You don't love me, Lord, but I know that You do because,

3. *When I fell down, You were there to pick me up.*"

The reason a parent can "fall seven times, and rise again" (Proverbs 24:16) is because He will be there to lift you up if you call upon Him for help. But there is little He can do when we will not admit that we have fallen. Of the miserable state of his people in Egypt, God told Moses, "I have heard them crying out . . . so I have come down to rescue them" (Exodus 3:7, 8).

It makes little sense to me that we wait so long to confess our humanity and need for help when He stands ready to marshal all the forces of Heaven to come to our aid. Pride is a hard taskmaster and robs us of resources that a parent of teenagers must have. Sometimes it is as if we are stubbornly holding on to our pathetic, little brown paper bag containing a limp, bologna sandwich when God is offering us a marvelous banquet feast. Likewise, our inability to swallow our pride before our teens and make the first move toward reconciliation with them might be keeping us from a "family-agape feast."

Elizabeth Elliot once wrote to her daughter,

Who is it you marry? You marry a sinner. There's nobody else to marry. . . . Acceptance of him—all of him—includes acceptance of his being a sinner. He is a fallen creature in need of the same kind of redemption all the rest of us are in need of. What a lot of heartbreak would be avoided if we could concentrate on the

*essentials and skip the rest. How much more we could
relax with one another and enjoy all there is to enjoy.*[1]

Parents and teens would do well to remember this advice
when tempted to hold grudges or harbor bad feelings for one
another. Two fundamentals for emancipating our teenagers
are judiciously giving them room to fail and experience the
consequences of their decisions, and honestly admitting our
own faults in their presence.

It is a liberating feeling to know that someone important
to you still loves you (in fact, may love you even more) in
spite of their awareness of your weaknesses. Driving to a
friend's home during summer vacation, I was reminded by
my wife of the major reason I love to be with my family.
After getting us hopelessly lost in the northern woods of
Michigan, I finally relented and pulled into a gas station for
new directions. I followed the station attendant's advice for a
few miles, but then my stubbornness flared up and I
announced that we were going to try a different "shortcut"
that I was sure would work. The moaning of Joyce and my
teens only deepened my resolve to redeem myself.

It wasn't long before I was looking for moss on the trees
and peering for familiar constellations. It was humiliating to
have to pull into another station and get a different set of
directions. This time, I drove in silence, and my family was
wise enough not to break it.

After sorting out my emotions and reflecting on my
juvenile behavior, I finally admitted, "You know what really
bothers me about this whole thing? It's not just that I got us
lost, or even that I'm responsible for wasting so much of our
vacation time. You guys know what it is, don't you?"

Their reply was more silence, but I had to finish. "It's
that you, my own family, saw me act like an absolute jerk
back there!"

That was it. I would say no more and they knew it. My

wife waited an appropriate amount of time, then reached over to pat me on the shoulder and spoke for the whole family: "That's okay, honey. We already knew you were like that."

There is no freedom like being loved by someone who really knows you.

"O Lord, you have searched me and you know me
(Psalm 139:1).
You are familiar with all my ways (Psalm 139:3).
Your love, O Lord, endures forever" (Psalm138:8).

We have come quite a distance together in this book. For two reasons I have great hope for you as the parent of a teenager: because you care, and because you can do all things through Christ who strengthens you.

I leave you with a final thought which summarizes much of what has gone before. I have asked many youth pastors in the past decade, "What is the biggest problem you face in ministering to teens?" Time and again I have heard them reply, "Parents with little faith in Christ and little time for their teens."

This situation does not have to be. Christian parents can be their teenagers' greatest asset. But teens will continue to leave the church if parents and the church do not pull together and work at eliminating barriers to the faith of their teens. And that takes time. I have a friend who wrote the following words to a famous old hymn of the church.

I ran today where Jesus walked, in days of long ago.
Raced down each little path He knew
I've a schedule as, you know.
I'm always busy,
I keep the pace
I hurry everywhere.
I ran today where Jesus walked.
And missed His presence there.

Footnotes

Preface
1. Dennis Miller, "Christian Teenagers: They're Leaving the Flock," *Moody Monthly*, September 1982.
2. Ibid.
3. Ibid.

Chapter 2
1. David A. Roozen, "Church Dropouts: Changing Patterns of Disengagement and Re-entry." *Review of Religious Research*, 21, No. 4 (Fall 1980), p. 427.
2. Judith Marks, "Teens and Religion." *Teen*. November 1980, p. 40.
3. Tipper Gore, *Raising PG Kids in an X-rated Society*, Abingdon Press, Nashville, Tenn., 1987, p. 103.
4. Ibid.
5. Barbara Hargrove and Stephen D. Jones, *Reaching Youth Today*, Valley Forge, Penn.: Judson Press, 1983, p. 53.
6. Roger Dudley, *Youth Perceptual Inventory*, Andrews University, Berrien Springs, Michigan, 1977.

Chapter 3
1. Donald Sloat, *The Dangers of Growing Up in a Christian Home*, Nashville, Tenn.: Thomas Nelson Publishing, 1987, p. 33.

2. Fred Feretti, "Are Teens Turning to Religion?" *Seventeen,* November 1980, p. 137.
3. Oswald Chambers, *My Utmost for His Highest,* p. 210.

Chapter 4

1. Franky Schaeffer, *A Time for Anger: The Myth of Neutrality,* Westchester, Ill. Crossway Books, 1982, p. 28.
2. Ibid.
3. Ibid. pp. 56-57.
4. Richard Fredericks, "A Manual Containing Information & Instruction on How to Conduct the Seminar, "Television and the Christian Family." Ph.D. project for the course, "Seminar in Religious Education Curriculum," Andrews University, 1981.
5. George Will, quoted in *Campus Life,* April 1984, p. 41.
6. Fredericks, p. 37.1
7. Mick Jagger, quoted in *Newsweek,* December 19, 1983, p. 92.
8. Boy George quoted in *Campus Life,* April 1984, p. 40.
9. Steve Smith quoted in *Circus,* October 1982.
10. Peter Chris quoted in *Rolling Stone,* April 7, 1977, p. 49.
11. Prince quoted in *Rolling Stone,* Feb. 19, 1981, pp. 54-55.
12. David Lee Roth quoted in *Rolling Stone,* Sept. 4, 1980, pp. 9-10.
13. Toab Hooper, quoted in *Primetime,* vol. 1, Winter 1986, p. 12.
14. Tipper Gore, *Raising PG Kids in an X-Rated Society,* pp. 109-110.
15. Mark Kelly quoted in *Primetime,* vol. 1, Winter 1986, p. 12.
16. Fredericks, p. 38

Chapter 5

1. T.R. Torkelson, "Sick of Hypocrisy," *Signs of the Times* 97 (March 1970): pp. 3-4, 70.
2. Marvin Powell, *Psychology of Adolescence,* New York: Holt, Rinehart and Winston, 1970, p. 288.
3. Benjamin Keeley, "Generations in Tension," *Review of Religious Research,* 17 (Spring 1976), pp. 221-22.
4. Virginia Gibbon, quoted in *PTA Magazine,* 1986, p. 179.

5. Robert F. Peck and Robert J. Havighurst, *The Psychology of Character Development*, New York: John Wiley and Sons, 1960, p. 180.

Chapter 6

1. Merton Strommen, *Five Cries of Youth*, New York: Harper and Row, 1974.
2. Craig Ellison, "Lonely Teens." *Christian Herald*, May 1979, pp. 15-18.
3. Elizabeth Hurlock, *Developmental Psychology: A Life-Span Approach*, 5th edition, New York: McGraw-Hill Book Company, 1980, p. 228.
4. Ibid. pp. 117, 187.
5. Stanley Coopersmith, *The Antecedents of Self-Esteem*, San Francisco, Calif.: W.H. Freeman, 1967, p. 163.
6. L. Joseph Stone and Joseph Church, *Childhood and Adolescence*, New York, Random House, 1957, p. 126.
7. William Bernard, *Human Development in Western Culture*, p.399.
8. Roger Dudley, *Why Teenagers Reject Religion*, Washington, D.C., Review and Herald Publishing Association, 1978, p.112.
9. Zig Ziglar, *Raising Positive Kids in a Negative World*, Oliver Nelson Publishing, Nashville, Tenn.: 1985, p. 158.
10. Ibid p. 158.

Chapter 7

1. Dan Spader, "Tired of Band-Aid Approaches to Youth Work?" *Moody Monthly*, January 1984, p. 55.
2. Michael Mason, "Faith Development of Young People," D. Min. final project, San Francisco Theological Seminary, 1984, p. 112.

Chapter 8

1. Josh McDowell, *Network News*, Fall 1987, Vol. V, No. 3.
2. Results of Seventeen survey, quoted in *Battle Plan*, November 1, 1987, Nashville, Tenn. p. 1.
3. Josh McDowell, *Network News*, p. 8.
4. Elizabeth Hurlock, *Developmental Psychology*, p. 247.
5. Ibid., p. 231.

6. N. Stinnett and S. Taylor, Parent-Child Relationships, *Journal of Genetic Psychology,* 1976, p. 105.
7. Bruce Narramore, *Adolescence Is Not an Illness,* Old Tappan, New Jersey: Fleming Revell, 1980, pp. 32-33.
8. Larry Richards, "The Hardest Test at School: When Your Teen's Values Are Challenged," *Parents & Teenagers,* edited by Jay Kesler, Wheaton, Ill., Victor Books, 1984, pp. 629-30.
9. Ernest Smith, *American Youth Culture: Group Life In Teenage Society,* New York: Free Press of Glencoe, 1962, pp. 182-3.

Chapter 9
1. Ernest Ligon, *Dimensions of Character,* New York, MacMillan, 1956, p. 105.
2. Elizabeth Hurlock, *Adolescent Development,* New York, McGraw-Hill, 1982, p. 444.
3. Diana Baumrind, *Current Patterns of Parental Authority,* American Psychological Association, 1971, pp. 200-251.
4. Samuel Southard, *People Need People,* Philadelphia, Penn., The Westminster Press, 1970, p. 126.
5. Roger Dudley, *Why Teenagers Reject Religion,* p. 49.

Chapter 10
1. Robert Grinder, *Adolescence,* New York, John Wiley and Sons, 1973, pp. 399-400.
2. William Rogers, *The Alienated Student,* Nashville, Tenn.: Board of Education, The United Methodist Church, 1969, p. 263.
3. Bruce Narramore, *Adolescence Is Not an Illness,* p. 130.
4. Dorothy Rogers, *The Psychology of Adolescence,* 3rd Ed., New York: Appleton Century Crofts, 1978, p. 237.
5. David Augsburger, *Witness Is Withness,* Chicago, Ill.: Moody Press, 1971, pp. 7-10.
6. C.S. Lewis, *That Hideous Strength,* New York: The MacMillan Company, 1946, p. 234.

Chapter 11
1. Bruce Barton, *The Man Nobody Knows,* New York: The MacMillan Company, 1952, p. 6.

2. Merton Strommen, *Bridging the Gap*, Minneapolis, Minn. Augsburg Publishing House, 1973, p. 165.
3. David Bresler, *Hugging Can Improve Your Health*, Andrews University.
4. Helen Colton, *The Joy of Touching*, New York: Seaview/Putnam, 1983, p. 148.
5. Kahil Gibran, *The Prophet*, New York: Alfred A. Knopf, 1975, p. 59.
6. Merton Strommen, *Five Cries of Youth*, New York, Harper & Row, 1974, p. 116.

Chapter 12
1. Urie Brofenbrenner, "The Origins of Alienation," *Scientific American*, Vol. 231, August 1974, p. 60.

Chapter 13
1. Elisabeth Elliot, *Growing Together*, September 1982, p. 6.